BIG LIFE LESSONS FROM THAT STILL, SMALL VOICE

A collection of stories
by Lisa Mason

INFINITY
PUBLISHING

ISBN 0-7414-6386-5

Printed in the United States of America

Published February 2011

INFINITY PUBLISHING
1094 New DeHaven Street, Suite 100
West Conshohocken, PA 19428-2713
Toll-free (877) BUY BOOK
Local Phone (610) 941-9999
Fax (610) 941-9959
Info@buybooksontheweb.com
www.buybooksontheweb.com

INTRODUCTION

I feel it is always best to lay one's cards on the table. No matter what the subject, honesty is the best policy. So, as it pertains to this little book, here goes. Here are my cards. I have very little authority to write it. I have no formal religious training. I have never been to the mission field. Truth be told, I am not even a very good Christian. But, I do have one thing going for me, and I guess that is the most important thing.

You see, about a year ago, I completed a course on gerontology. Yes, the study of old people. Yes, depressing. But, I digress. Anyway, I learned that if the statistics are correct, I am already more than halfway around the track. Fifty percent of my life is over. Gone. Never to be returned. And, that's only if I live to the full age expectancy of eighty-four without cancer or a car wreck getting in the way.

It's funny about that idea of halfway. With it comes an almost impossible-to-ignore urge to look back on the first half and see how it went. Kind of like the halftime report during a football game. So, I did my own halftime report. I tried to remember the people who had come in and out of my life and the lessons that I had learned. I wrote them all down so that I would not forget them.

And that's when I figured out what I had going for me. You see, despite the fact that I am not a theologian or a crusader, God has never given up on me. He has never stopped whispering encouragements, never stopped nudging me out of harm's way, and never stopped pricking my conscience when I did wrong. He has always been there. And, maybe, that is the very point. You don't have to be an expert to know about God. You just have to listen. So, for what it's worth, here are my big life lessons from God's still, small voice.

Revelation1:11 ...What thou seest, write in a book...

ONE:

Finding Wisdom.

Childhood. A subject I had not thought about in a very long time. And, probably wouldn't have, had I not run across the picture that day. Frankly, I'm surprised I noticed it at all, given my frenzied state. Financial documents of every type littered my living room, all waiting to be searched, sorted, and stacked before being transported to the accountant's office. It was an annual task I dreaded, but never more so than that year. That very bad year. That year of bank failures, home foreclosures, and disappearing 401K plans. Even without our accountant's final analysis, my husband and I knew our loss would be substantial. I surveyed the mess.

"How will we get through this?" I asked aloud to no one. I sighed heavily. All I really wanted to do was sleep.

It was then that I saw the corner of a photograph peeking out from between two bank statements. I bent over, intending to free it, when I noticed that the two documents were stuck together and the picture was stuck between them. I have always found it perplexing that papers, merely sitting in a cardboard box, can somehow become "glued" together. But, they were "glued" all the same, so I slowly peeled them apart, careful not to tear the photo.

Finally, it was free. A 4x4 black-and-white snapshot of two little girls, their arms around each other's shoulders, grinning like idiots into the camera. One girl was considerably larger than the other. I turned it over to the back. A handwritten scribble indicated the year 1969. I turned it back to the front and looked again.

"Good Lord, were you really that chubby?" I asked aloud to no one. I moved a stack of papers from the coffee table and dropped the picture there. I cleared a place for myself on the couch to lie down. My mind was exhausted with worry, my body depressed. I closed my eyes.

****

1969.

I awoke with a start and glanced cautiously around. Safe. No one had noticed that I fell asleep. I wiped the side of my mouth with the back of my hand, just to be sure that I hadn't drooled, and prepared to settle back into semi-slumber when I felt a sharp pinch on my left forearm. I snapped my head around to the offender and found myself eye-to-eye with my older sister, Missy. At nine years of age, she was already terribly bossy.

"I'm telling!" she mouthed the words. Missy dared not speak aloud since whispering in church was an even bigger offense than taking the occasional siesta. I kicked her ankle with my leather Sunday shoe and scooted away. I slid easily on the wooden pew and wondered briefly how many butts had skimmed across that very bench over the years, with all of the Sunday morning services, Sunday evening services, weddings, funerals, etc. But I quickly dismissed the attempt to calculate since, at the ripe old age of seven, I decided that mathematics, of any type, was totally unnecessary in life. I looked straight ahead, ignored her scowls, and willed myself to stay awake. The pastor preached passionately from the pulpit, his voice filling the tiny Baptist church sanctuary, his arms waving above his head.

"Now is the time!" he proclaimed. "Search your heart. Receive Jesus today!" My daddy. He was WOUND up. I scanned the sanctuary and spotted Mama. She sat on the front row and looked up at Daddy, Bible on her lap. Only recently had she allowed Missy and me to sit by ourselves in church. I preferred to sit in the very back of the church. There, I could draw pictures of horses with flowing manes and tails. My perfect sister, on the other hand, wanted to sit up front "in case Mother needs us." What a big suck-up. We compromised and sat in the middle.

The tiny, rural Texas church was uncomfortably hot that Sunday in late October. It was after twelve o'clock and the temperature reached the upper eighties, not uncommon for Texas, even well into the autumn months. All around me older women fanned themselves vigorously, cardboard handheld fans swished to and fro. It reminded me of windshield wipers on high speed. Occasionally, I caught a whiff of Wrigley's Juicy Fruit gum mingled with old-lady toilet water. My daddy continued his impassioned pleas for lost souls, inspired by the congregation.

"Amen, Amen, Pastor!" said the men in the congregation. They fanned their faces with their hats, the cowboy variety. Actually, the whole congregation was made up of old people, or so it seemed to me.

I tried to focus on Daddy's words, but I was just too bored. I preferred sermons that had stories associated with them. Daniel and the lions' den was a good one. I visualized it easily and it had a good ending. Noah and the ark was also a favorite. I especially liked my version. In it, the animals loaded onto the ark included two pure white horses. They were, of course, named Snowball I and Snowball II. But my most loved story was when Jesus fed thousands of followers with just a few loaves and fishes. Although, for some reason, whenever I pictured this event, the loaves dripped with garlic and butter and the fishes glistened, golden brown, from the fat they had just been fried in.

My stomach growled very, very loudly. I cautiously cut my eyes over at my sister to see if she had heard. Yep, no doubt about it. I scooted further away from her, indignant. Did I have any control over my healthy, digestive juices? I thought of Mama's waiting lunch and willed Daddy to give the altar call. But he was still wrapped up tight in the Holy Spirit, so we wouldn't be going anywhere for a long while.

I sighed heavily. I did not care if my prissy sister heard as I thought of the extraordinary pot roast that waited to be taken from the oven. It had simmered since early that morning, surrounded by sweet baby carrots, freshly peeled potatoes, and whole succulent onions. Although we had very little money, we had plenty of good food, thanks to the members of my daddy's church and their overflowing gardens and barns. The mere thought of the midday bounty caused my salivary glands to fire in a frenzy. For the second time that day, I wiped the side of my mouth with the back of my hand, just to be sure.

I tried to catch my daddy's eye. I thought I could point to a make-believe wristwatch on my arm. Sort of like *wind it up, Pops,* but I thought better of it and realized I would just have to wait out the Godly storm taking place in the pulpit. Finally, the altar call was given. Those who wanted to be saved went up front, whispered to my daddy, prayed, and then returned to their seats.

Glory, Glory Alleluia, the service was over, souls were saved, and it was time for food! I bolted from the church and thought only of nourishment. The meal was even more delicious than I imagined. A roast, vegetables, fresh biscuits, and apple cobbler. I filled my stomach to the brim and grew drowsy. I excused myself from the table while Mama and Missy cleaned up. I went into the bedroom I shared with my sister and lay down on my side of the bed. I listened to the sounds of dishes being washed and silverware being put away. After a few minutes, I heard my sister approach our bedroom. I closed my eyes quickly. I pretended that I was asleep.

"I know you're awake," she said. I continued to play possum.

"Come on, let's go outside and play!" she said. No way, sister.

"We can make mud pies," she continued, "you can be the hostess and I will be the customer!"

The idea tempted me, since this was one of my favorite games to play, but still no dice. Although my eyes remained closed, I knew exactly what she was doing. At that moment, she had crossed her arms tightly across her tiny chest. Soon, she would tap that little foot of hers.

"How about if I read to you?" she asked. She knew this was my true weakness.

I cracked one eyelid and looked up at her. "*Little House,*" I said, "the Christmas part." I quickly snapped my eye shut and didn't wait for a response. She read of Laura Ingalls Wilder and her sister, Mary, and how they made Christmas candy. She was a very good reader. She did different voices for each character and never missed a word. Maybe she wasn't such a suck-up. After all, she hadn't told Daddy that I had fallen asleep during his sermon or that I had kicked her. I listened intently, as images of holiday candy, brightly colored packages, and Baby Jesus in the manger flooded my mind. As I did, I realized that

Christmas wasn't that far off. The summer was over. But what a summer it had been!

It all started when my daddy moved us to Texas. He felt he was being called to become a minister, and although he had been ordained in his home state of Tennessee, he knew that to continue his spiritual work, he would need to further his education. So, Daddy moved our little family, lock, stock, and barrel. Our destination was a tiny church in Maypearl, Texas, in close proximity to Southwestern Theological Seminary in Fort Worth. That was where he would go to school.

After several days of driving, we arrived in Maypearl. We discovered that the pastor's house sat on a dirt road, directly across from a cotton field. In the middle of that field was a cotton gin. The gin churned throughout the day and night and spewed remnants of cotton into the air. The hum of machinery was ever present. Down the dirt road from our house was the Negro Baptist Church. Daddy became friends with the pastor of that church and offered to help in any way possible. The reverend from the Negro Baptist Church offered the same to my daddy.

Daddy loved the people in his congregation. They were poor but generous. In fact, most times, the pay for my daddy came in the form of vegetables from someone's garden or hand-me-down clothes from someone's attic. He especially loved old Mr. and Mrs. Dawson. They were the eldest people in my daddy's church and really liked my parents. Often, they let us work in their huge vegetable patch and load up all that we could carry. Afterward, Mrs. Dawson invited us to their back porch to "sit a spell." She always treated us to an icy-cold Dr Pepper in a bottle.

Soon, Daddy started school. He took our car with him, so Mama, Missy, and I found ourselves on foot. One day, Mama found a bicycle in someone's trash heap. It sat by the side of the road and was obviously meant to be thrown away. It was a man's model, absolutely huge, with a long flat area that ran atop the back wheel. The frame was bent and it was covered in rust, but Mama decided it was better than nothing, so she brought it home. Every day, Mama loaded Missy on the front handlebars and me on the back. Off she pedaled the half mile to the tiny downtown to get mail from the post office or food from the market. I hung on for dear life as the bent frame rubbed against the tire. It made a loud *scrape-scrape-scrape* noise and caused tiny flecks of rust to flutter through the air like burgundy confetti.

And so it went. Daddy at school every day, and Missy and I at home with Mama and our bicycle. That is until the July 4th Baptist picnic. That's when we met the new family that joined our church. And, not just any family, but one that had a set of twins. Well, people spoke of those twins with such awe and reverence that Missy and I wanted to be a part of their elite group. And while it might seem improbable that two girls, several years apart in age, could be mistaken for twins, it actually wasn't that far-fetched. Here's why. Missy was extremely thin and I was, well, hefty. I came into this world with a healthy appetite and quickly overtook my sister in the weight department. So, although my heft came in handy in our quest for twin-dom, we knew we had one more hurdle to overcome before achieving our goal.

You see, Missy had poker-straight, thin hair. I, however, had the most beautiful head of Shirley Temple curls you had ever laid eyes on. So, we realized that our hair also needed to match if we were to be perfect twins. We pestered Mama relentlessly. After several days of the harassment, she finally broke down and scraped together the ninety-nine cents to buy a home permanent kit from a dollar store. Mama took a chair from the dining room and brought it into the kitchen. She put newspapers down on the floor under the chair to catch the spillage and borrowed several phone books from the neighbors for Missy to sit on. Mama read the instructions and then wrapped Missy's hair around the plastic wands provided in the Toni home perm box. After that, she squirted on a solution that smelled like rotten eggs. I ran from the kitchen, held my nose, and screamed at the top of my lungs.

"Missy smells like farts! Missy smells like farts!" Missy laughed and Mama reminded her to keep her head still as the solution was squirted. Mama had put a bath towel around Missy's neck, secured with a clothespin. But Missy slipped around so much on the numerous phone books that the clothespin popped off. Missy squealed bloody murder, as the cold solution ran down her back.

Finally, the timer was set so that the neutralizing lotion could be applied at precisely the right moment. As we waited for the lotion to be applied and the rollers to be removed, Missy and I gazed upon the picture on the Toni box. The girl on the box had the most perfect head of curls. She smiled ear to ear as she scampered through a field of flowers. Our little minds went wild as we imagined our lives as twins. We whispered to each other of the adventures we would have, as Mama started to remove the curlers. She tossed the curlers into the sink, each one made a *clink* sound as it hit the porcelain. We held our breath with excitement.

"Oh dear, oh dear!" Mama exclaimed. Unfortunately, she had not rolled the rods up high enough on Missy's head. As a result, her head looked just like a steeple, pointed on the top and hugely round across the bottom, not at all like the Toni girl on the box. Missy cried. Mama promised to get another perm and try again the next day. In the meantime, she told my sister that she could wear a scarf around her head. Missy put the scarf on her head and attempted to tie the two ends together snugly under her chin. Unfortunately, that just made the sides and the back of her hair bulge out even more. I looked at her. My sister looked just like a giant blowfish. I told her so. She cried harder.

Mama bought another perm and tried again. She rolled, squirted, and unrolled. This time, she made sure that the curlers were rolled up nice and high. Unfortunately, not enough time had passed since the first perm, and the results were just as disastrous. Only one side of my sister's head took. Missy cried and again reached for the scarf. This time, she looked like a blowfish on one side and a pancake on the other. Not to be defeated, Mama tried several more times. Finally, it happened. The Toni home perm came out beautifully. In that brief moment, we were twins. And, the timing was perfect. You see, I always dreamed of starting first grade with my perfect twin at my side.

The morning finally arrived. Missy waited patiently for me by the front door of our house. She insisted on walking me the few blocks to school. She wanted to show me my classroom. She was going into third grade and was already quite experienced with the layout of the schoolhouse. It was a huge, brick structure and all twelve grades were housed in the same building. As we approached the schoolyard, we saw boys and girls of all ages clustered together. They laughed happily and got reacquainted after the summer vacation.

We entered the front doors of the school. Missy gave me my milk money and told me to put it in my pocket and not take it out until lunch. Mama had given Missy two nickels that morning with the strict instructions that Missy was to carry them both and not give me mine until we were at school. They were both afraid I would lose my nickel.

Missy took me inside the school and led me down a central hallway. On both sides of the hall, classroom doors were open. As I glanced inside, I saw teachers and students alike, as they got ready for homeroom. At the end of the hallway was my classroom. Missy took me inside and showed me where to sit down. I was the first student to arrive. Missy told me to stay put and wait for my teacher. I nodded. She told me to meet her at that very spot at the end of the day. She would walk me home, she said. She left.

I looked around. The room had a very high ceiling. It was dimly lit and very cool. The huge blackboard proclaimed the word "welcome." In front of the blackboard was a massive wooden desk and on that desk sat stacks and stacks of books. They were well worn, their spines broken from years of use, images of Dick and Jane on the front cover. Inside the back cover was a handwritten list of boys and girls who had been assigned those very books in previous school years. The list included notations of when the books had been given out and when they had been returned. And each notation was signed by Mrs. Lansford, my first-grade teacher.

She was about sixty years old or so. Round, wire-rimmed glasses sat atop her nose and framed her blue eyes. Her short, gray hair was beautifully styled, each curl in place. A #2 pencil was nestled just over her ear, supported by Aqua Net and just the right amount of teasing. That day, she brought vanilla cupcakes to school. On top was pink icing for the girls, blue icing for the boys. She hugged me when I left. Her cheek felt like velvet.

At the end of the school day, just as she promised, my sister came to my classroom. She said it was time to walk home. I tucked my *Dick and Jane* book under my arm and chatted about the boys and girls in my class.

"You have some pink icing on your lip," Missy said as we walked.

"We had a cupcake party!" I said.

"How many did you have?" she asked.

"One." I lied. She didn't say anything. Just walked and looked straight ahead.

"Three." I admitted. I dropped my head in shame. She took my hand, her tiny forearm pressed against my meaty one. I looked up. She smiled.

"I'll read to you when we get home," she said. My heart lifted.

We read together almost every evening after that. It became a welcome respite from the other events I witnessed.

Like when my daddy had worried, sleepless nights, when the offering plate was empty. And when my mama had knots of fear when I had one of my bad headaches and there was no money for a doctor.

Or when I slapped a little boy on the face after he said that my sister and I were poor.

Or when I heard a group of white teenage boys yell the N word to the cotton-field workers across the dirt road from our house.

I wanted to scream out, "Shut up! I'll kill you!" but because I was a preacher's kid, I couldn't act out. So, I stomped through the house with all my might and went into the bedroom I shared with my sister. I lay down on my side of the bed and cried. Later, Mama came into our room. She sat down on the bed beside me. She didn't say a word; she just rubbed my back. But, she knew. Somehow, she knew.

****

13

The tear that ran down my cheek startled me. I wiped it off impatiently and got up from the couch. I surveyed the financial documents still scattered around my living room but, this time, with much less fear. Because those documents represented only money. Just money. Money I had lived without for most of my life. Money I could live without again.

From the coffee table, two precious faces smiled up at me. Little warriors, I realized, grinning through it all. Part of a poor, insignificant family that simply refused to give up, refused to lose their faith. What my family had lived through humbled me. My husband and I would be fine. We would be just fine.

I thought about framing the little picture, but decided against it. Instead, I put it back in the box that housed my financial documents. Who knows? I might need it again in the future. That's the thing about memory lane. When you travel down it, you never know what you will bring back. Sometimes, laughter. Sometimes, tears. And, sometimes, if you are very, very lucky, God sends you back with a little bit of wisdom.

Big Life Lesson Number One: Sometimes, you have to look to the past to find wisdom for the future.

Two:

Growing Up.

I was at a charity luncheon event in New York City recently. You know the kind. Forced to sit at a specified table and eat a mediocre meal with a person you've never laid eyes on before. It was there that I met a lady by the name of Deidre. Over the mixed-greens-with-tons-of-Thousand-Island-salad-dressing course, I learned that she had lived her entire life in Connecticut. Her childhood home sat on five and a half acres, overlooking the countryside. Her parents still owned the home, she said. She went there every holiday. Over the undercooked chicken cordon bleu course, she told me of her educational background. It seemed that she had attended a wonderful private Catholic school, K through 12, and then went on to Brown and later Harvard. She and her sorority sisters still got together at least once a year, she said.

And then, apparently realizing that she had monopolized the entire conversation, she asked me about my accent.

"Southern," I answered.

"Really?" she said, suddenly interested. "Where did you grow up?" I could practically read her mind as she readied herself for my stories of genteel sophistication, old money, and magnolia trees.

"Well, let's see," I said, buying time. How would I explain my unconventional growing-up years to such a refined lady?

Just then, the waiter whisked away our cordon bleu plates. The keynote speaker was making her way to the podium. It was time for quiet.

"Maybe I'll get to hear your story another time," she whispered, leaning over to me. I nodded, knowing full well I would never see her again. Probably for the best.

****

"Load up the boxes, Barb!" my daddy yelled. "We're moving again!" Hopefully, you have already met my daddy (Paul), my mama (Barbara), and my big sister (Missy). The three people I began my life with. In the beginning, we lived in Texas, just the four of us. My father was a minister. He pastored a small Baptist church and dutifully led his flock. It was the perfect foursome. I thought it would last forever. Boy, was I wrong.

Little brother Christopher Micah arrived shortly after I entered second grade. All boy, he had the richest brown eyes of any baby I had ever seen. He came into this world with a healthy appetite and a healthy pair of lungs to match. He ruled the house and we doted on him terribly.

Two years later, little brother Matthew Henry arrived. A quiet baby, he had sparkling blue eyes and a beautiful face. He was loving and very accommodating. He played quietly for hours and never disturbed anyone. We doted on him equally.

So, there we were in Texas. Two girls, two boys, a mama, and a daddy settled in for the long haul, or so I thought. But remember, Daddy was a minister, and as a result, he felt that we should be prepared to move at a moment's notice. He said one just never knew when the Holy Spirit would call. Interesting fact: My daddy seemed to be the only person in our family who ever **actually heard** the voice of the Holy Spirit. Try as I might, I couldn't even get a whisper.

So, over the next several years, that's what we did. Move. A lot. My poor mama. She finally just stopped throwing cardboard boxes away, knowing full well she would need them again in a few months' time. She flattened down the boxes and put them in the basement or attic. The boxes had words like "kitchen utensils," "bathroom toiletries," or "kids bedroom" written all over them in different places. But I'm getting ahead of myself.

From that beginning point in Texas we moved to Georgia. Our first stop, Thompson, Georgia. A small town in the southern part of the state, Daddy found work at a little country church. The church sat on top of a hill, surrounded by thick trees. A steep gravel road led up to the church. The pastor's house, where we lived, sat at the bottom of the hill. You could always tell if someone was going up to the church. The crunch of gravel under their car tires was very loud.

It was in Thompson that I developed my first crush on a boy. His name was Glenn and I thought he was perfect. He was several years older than I was when I first spotted him. I guessed him to be about fourteen. I slipped out during afternoon choir practice one day. It was late August and the evening sun that streamed through the sanctuary windows tempted me to take a break. Besides, I already knew the song. Also, I was tired of the girl who sang alto and sat next to me. She had obviously not brushed her teeth that day. Oh, the smell.

I walked outside to the front of the church and heard the crunch of gravel. Someone was on the other side of the building. I peeked around and saw him. He smoked a cigarette. I watched, enthralled, as he inhaled and then blew out a perfect smoke ring. He wore a white tee shirt tucked into straight-leg

Wrangler's, his shaggy hair perfectly tipped with highlights. Yes, this is love, I decided. I turned and went back into choir practice. I knew I would soon be missed. I watched him for several weeks and discovered that (gasp) he already had a girlfriend. Her name was Dawn. She also had perfectly highlighted hair, was super thin, and also wore Wrangler's. No wonder I didn't know about her. I thought she was his sister. It was about a month later, after evening services, that I followed him as he walked to his parents' car. Maybe I could talk him out of being in love with Dawn. I tried to walk lightly so that he wouldn't hear the crunch of the gravel under my feet. He got closer and closer to his parents' car and I realized that I needed to get his attention. I wanted to call out, but my throat had closed up completely. I looked down at my feet and got an idea. I picked up a pebble and threw it at him. Nothing. I picked up a larger pebble and tossed it. Nothing. Before he got too far away, I picked up a golf-ball-sized rock and hurled it. I hit him square in the back. He whipped around and looked at me with such contempt that I flung myself into a nearby ditch.

"What are you doing?" he yelled, stroking his highlighted hair. I said nothing, just stared. He was so beautiful.

"Are you crazy?" he said. "What are you doing in the ditch?" I panicked.

"I was practicing in case a tornado comes by," I said. I had just learned about that in school.

He paused for a minute and looked down at me. Lying on my back, moisture was beginning to seep into my shirt from the wet mud in the ditch. Soon, other church members would exit from the church and go to their cars. I had to get up. This could be embarrassing. I held my hand up toward him so that he could assist me. He just looked at me and walked away. So much for love. He could go back to Dawn, for all I cared.

Thank goodness, the Holy Spirit called again shortly thereafter.

We left Thompson, Georgia for Sylvester, Georgia. Another small town, but a bigger church. It was also in Sylvester that another Mason was added to the family. Baby sister Amanda Teal was born. Absolutely gorgeous, she was the apple of everyone's eye. Chubby cheeks, brown eyes, and always happy. I fell madly in love the first time I held her. So, there we were in Sylvester. Three girls, two boys, Mama and Daddy, and a church that wasn't sitting on a dirt road or a gravel path. Surely we would settle down now, I thought. Not so much.

You see, pastors preached at other churches or spoke at church conferences. And, in our case, that meant that the whole family had to attend. Oftentimes, these events were held in other states. So we did what any smart family would do to avoid high hotel bills. We bought a camper. No, not the luxurious type that had a bathroom and shower onboard. No, my daddy felt that the Holy Spirit wanted us to have a secondhand pop-up. Another interesting fact: The Holy Spirit also seemed to communicate with my daddy about his choice of vehicles. Once he felt led to buy an old Volvo, but when it stopped running after only two weeks, Daddy said he must have misunderstood the Holy Spirit.

Back to the pop-up. I don't know who invented this vehicle, but I can assure you that he, or she, was not one of several children crammed into this ever-morphing structure. Oh, the moments of frustration as my mama attempted to push out the sides and back end of the pop-up. She struggled to lock them down so that we could go to bed. And then, of course, there was the necessary choreography at bedtime. You see, the weight had to be equally distributed on all ends of the pop-up or it would tilt over during the night. So, Daddy stood outside the camper and yelled instructions to Mama as to which child should move where. When it became apparent that space was a problem in the pop-up, Mama came up with a solution. She put all of our clothes in buckets. Clever really, when you realized that buckets could be easily stacked or conveniently hung from whatever makeshift hook was available. A tree branch, perhaps the edge of a car bumper. She labeled our buckets very clearly, but that did not stop me, in my laziness, from rustling around in the first bucket I came across. Many a time, on the way to the Christian campsite shower house, I discovered I clutched Fruit-of-the-Looms instead of girl panties.

So it went. My daddy preached at the church in Sylvester and traveled constantly for other commitments. We tagged along. Mama learned to stretch an already-stretched budget. She perfected the fine points of thrift-store shopping. She found great bargains, whipped off the twenty-five-cent sticker, washed the garments to a tee, and put them in our drawers (or buckets) before we ever knew what happened. I, frankly, loved the idea of moving, because with each new home came new adventures. So, when I learned that the Holy Spirit had given my daddy another shout-out, I was thrilled. We packed up and left Sylvester and made our way north, to just outside Atlanta.

Until that time, I had gone to relatively small schools. In Texas, all the grades were in one building. In the two other schools I attended, the elementary and high school buildings were separate, but the classes were tiny. This new school, however, was very different. It was huge. Absolutely huge. So, I began my eighth-grade year with much anticipation. I quickly discovered that my favorite subject was world geography. Not because I was particularly interested in the subject matter but because I was mesmerized by the teacher.

Her name was Ms. Thames. When I first got to class, I pronounced her name just as it was spelled. Thames, like names. She quickly corrected me.

"It is pronounced 'tims,' just like the river," she said. I looked at her in confusion. She explained that the River Thames was the second longest river in the UK, which, incidentally, was a country very close to France. You see, Ms. Thames was from France and, while the class was supposed to be about world geography, we never got very far out of France. For the entire year, we learned about French food, French politicians, French agriculture, French tourism, anything that had to do with France. Occasionally, we ventured over to Germany or Switzerland or Belgium, but only as it related as to how those countries got along with France.

She was so passionate about France that she actually organized a dinner for our class to go to a fancy French restaurant in downtown Atlanta. What a treat. That evening she wore a green silk dress and a beautiful gossamer scarf tied around her head. So very French. We were served several courses in the candle-lit restaurant, all twenty of us serious and somber due to such a grown-up event. At one point, Ms. Thames spoke privately with a very handsome French waiter. (I'm pretty sure they spoke French during that conversation.) In my fourteen-year-old mind, they planned a romantic rendezvous. In actuality, I later learned that she was just trying to wrangle free dessert for her students.

She was outrageously beautiful. A tiny woman, she had a streaming mane of red hair and always wore huge, round, green glasses. They were perfect on her petite face since they brought attention to her equally enormous green eyes. During class, she often took the glasses off her face and put them on top of her head. Her red hair, nestled in the bright-green glasses, made her look like a perfect Christmas ornament. Wow! Soon, I became determined to get those same glasses for myself. I wanted to be

Ms. Thames. French, tiny, and beautiful. But, I knew that my parents would never buy me those chic glasses unless they thought that I really needed them. So I came up with a plan. I squinted at the television, feigned headaches, and rubbed my eyes constantly. At first they kind of ignored me but finally Mama took the bait and got me an eye-doctor appointment. The day finally arrived for the appointment. I pictured how I would look in the Ms. Thames glasses. I imagined I would toss my hair and speak with a slight French accent. Mama went in with me into the exam room where I was asked to identify letters and numbers. During the course of the exam it became apparent that I really couldn't see that well. The doctor kept showing the letters and numbers bigger and bigger for me to read. Mama was informed that I was seriously nearsighted and needed glasses. We went to the lobby area where a collection of frames were displayed. There! I saw them! Huge, round, and green!

"I want these!" I exclaimed and put them on. Mama looked at me in dismay.

"Lisa," she said, "I don't think those are right for you." I looked at myself in the mirror and thought I looked fabulous. Of course I thought I looked fabulous. I was wearing frames with no lenses and I was blind as a bat.

I begged and begged and finally wore my mama down. She ordered the lenses and frames. We would be able to pick them up in two weeks' time. The time dragged but I used the days wisely. I fantasized about my glasses and how French I would look. I read books aloud to my little sister Amanda, and attempted to perfect my French accent. Finally, the day arrived for the Ms. Thames glasses to be delivered. We arrived at the eye doctor's office and were instructed to sit down at a counter with mirrors strategically placed in front of each chair. I was breathless with excitement. The doctor entered the room. He held my huge, round, green glasses.

"OK," he said, "let me put these on for you and make sure they fit properly."

"That's OK," I quickly replied. "I would like to do it myself!" I held out my hand expectantly. He laughed and handed them over to me. Of course the first thing I did was to put them on top of my head. My mama looked perplexed as I placed them carefully, just as one might place a crown during the final moments of the Miss America contest. I looked in the mirror. Spectacular!

I tried to take them off but discovered that the nosepieces were stuck in my hair. I tugged and felt some hair being ripped from my scalp. I hadn't planned on that happening. I would have to practice a lot to make sure that I could get them off in one smooth movement.

Finally, I put the glasses on properly and looked in the mirror. I prepared myself for French beauty, but what greeted me in the mirror could only be described as sheer horror. With the lenses in place, I saw for the first time what I really looked like. The huge, round, green glasses made me look like a toad. I already had a very round face and the glasses accentuated the shape. The hairs from my scalp were still caught in the nosepieces. They cascaded down my cheeks and tickled my nose. I sneezed. I looked in the mirror again to see red-rimmed bug eyes, a dripping nose, and hairy glasses. Not at all like Ms. Thames. I immediately took the glasses off. Literally, I took them off while we sat in the doctor's office and put them in their little case. That's where they stayed. I cried for several days. Then Micah and Matthew cried. Finally, my parents could stand the drama no longer. They bought me a different pair of frames. This time, Mama picked them out.

I finished my eighth-grade year and looked forward to high

school in Atlanta. But, I was told by my daddy that the Holy Spirit had other plans. We were moving again. This time, to an army base. Good Lord, not an army base! Surely the Holy Spirit had gotten His signals crossed! Daddy had been an army reservist for many years, so when a position opened up for him to become a full-time army chaplain, he took it. So, off we went to the Fort Sill army base in Lawton, Oklahoma, and what can only be described as very interesting housing. Boxy, squat, and beige, all of the houses in the compound looked the same to me, so for the first couple of weeks I walked around in confusion. I wasn't sure which house was ours.

My daddy suggested I find a job. After all, I was going on fifteen and constantly asked for money. The catch was that I didn't have a driver's license, so any job I found had to be within walking distance. In essence, I had to find a position on the army base. I checked the community bulletin board and discovered a position for an organist. Since I had played the piano from childhood, I figured that I could handle an organ, so I applied. When I got the job, I was thrilled. When I learned where it was, I wasn't so thrilled. I also found out why no one else had taken the position.

I arrived for my first Sunday engagement, songbook in hand. I walked into the building indicated on my employment sheet and checked in. Just like the residential buildings, this building was also boxy, squat, and beige, so I wasn't the least bit concerned. However, when I noticed the bars on the windows, I was. Yes, I was the organist for the jail. Although, when I turned my time sheet into the bursar's office, the receptionist handed it right back to me and asked me to fill out another one.

"Why?" I asked. I examined it more closely. I had put down the right dates and the right amount of money.

"It isn't a jail," she whispered loudly, pointing to my sheet where I had written the word *jail*, "it's a military stockade."

"Honey, if there are bars on the windows and folks are in handcuffs, it's a jail," I thought to myself. But, I changed my time sheet, anyway. I needed the dough. I continued to play at the jail, stockade, whatever. The money was good and the gig was easy. It seemed that all the men ever wanted to sing was "America the Beautiful" and "What a Friend We Have in Jesus." I realized that patriotism and Christianity was a winning combination, especially for the incarcerated.

All went well for a while. I went to Lawton High School along with my older sister, Missy. Micah and Matthew were in elementary school and Amanda, the baby, stayed at home with Mama. But then it happened. Yes, you guessed it. The Holy Spirit spoke. We moved again. But this time, it was different. It was international. Sweet Lord.

But first, a bit of background information. When the army flies you to a foreign country, it is generally done under what is called "space available." Basically, whatever plane is flying in your general direction is what you are going to ride on. And, that does not always include planes that were originally designed to carry people. So, when my mama learned that the army was flying us to Germany on a cargo aircraft, she was nervous. Daddy said not to worry. He said the plane would be converted so that we could travel comfortably. Well, we traveled. But not exactly in comfort.

First, there were the makeshift seats that faced backwards. Second, there were the earplugs that had to be used because of the loud engine noises. And, third, there was the Dramamine that had to be administered due to the fact that the plane was refueled during flight. Yes, refueled. Our plane slowed down over the Atlantic Ocean so that another plane could position its fuel hose into our tank. Oh, the nausea. At one point, I attempted to provide a bit of comic relief, so I took my yellow, spongy earplugs from my ears and put them up my nose. I motioned wildly for my family to look at me. I couldn't get their attention any other way, due to the noise. My little brothers squealed with delight and did the same thing. Mama, who had already vomited once and was in the act of doing it again, demanded that we all take our earplugs out of our nostrils and put them back in our ears. Daddy, who never experienced a moment of motion sickness in his life, slumbered through it all.

Finally, we touched down in Germany. We were assigned to the very remote village of Sögel, located in northern Germany. In fact, it was so remote that it was suggested that we take remedial German language classes, so that we could converse with the townspeople when necessary. We hastily learned what we could before we left Oklahoma.

When we arrived, we discovered it was exactly as we had anticipated. A beautiful, tiny hamlet with lovely homes and warm people. My daddy wanted to bridge the language barrier with our new neighbors so he encouraged us to use our German whenever possible. In all honesty, my German was a bit shaky so I stayed with the standard "Wo ist der bahnhof?" and "Pommes frites, bitta." Translated, "Where is the train station?" and "French fries, please!" I figured with these two phrases I could always find my way home and have a salty snack along the way. Frankly, all of us were a bit uncertain about our German. The language classes were spotty and we crammed in all we could in just a few sessions. But still we forged ahead. In fact, Daddy decided to use a bit of his German in the pulpit during one of his first sermons. I imagine he felt that it indicated proper respect to the people and the country who had invited us as temporary guests.

It was wintertime. Snow blanketed the area. It weighed down tree branches and clung to rooftops. It was everywhere, deep, white, and beautiful. So Daddy decided to use the snow as a parable of sorts. It went something like this. "Just as the warm sun will melt away the snow, so will God's forgiveness melt away our sins." It sounded wonderful, in theory. The problem was that Daddy didn't quite use the right German word for snow. Yes, the word started with an "s" but it wasn't snow he said. The church attendees looked bewildered as the sermon progressed. My daddy attempted to get his point across, so he used the S word with more vigor and gave the S word more emphasis. Still, there was confusion on the part of the parishioners. Imagine, to their ears my daddy declared, "Just as the warm sun will melt away our excrement, so will God's forgiveness melt away our sin."

After the sermon, my little sister Amanda innocently asked Daddy why he was saying the word s*** so much. She was the only one who had truly learned German. Daddy apologized for his unintended use of profanity. Our German friends forgave us. However, my daddy never attempted to be bilingual in the pulpit again.

****

I have to admit that for a time, as an adult, I avoided talking about my past. I told myself it was because it was just too complicated trying to explain it all but, deep down, I knew the truth.

I was ashamed of it. I had moved so many times that when people asked me where I grew up, I abruptly changed the subject. How could I possibly explain my nomadic life to them?

I wanted more than anything to be like Deidre, that lady I met in New York City at the charity lunch. She grew up in Connecticut with privilege and private schools, in a home that overlooked the countryside. I would never have that.

But, slowly, I began to understand that it is less about *where* you grew up and more about *how* you grew up. And that's when I grew up. Literally. And realized how proud I was of where I had come from. No, I would never have a traditional past, but I would have something much better. My past. So, for my somewhat strange, rather odd, hard-to-define growing-up years, I would like to thank the following: Daddy, Mama, siblings, Glenn, Ms. Thames, the boys in the jail (stockade), my German friends, and, of course, the Holy Spirit.

I wouldn't change a thing.

Big Life Lesson Number Two: It may not be perfect, but it is the only one you will ever have. Your past. Make peace with it.

THREE:

Fitting In.

Fitting in. That age-old, universally understood desire to be a part of a group or organization. Oftentimes, harmless. Sometimes, not so harmless.

****

I had just returned to the US from Germany. As you know, I lived briefly there with my family, but it was always the plan that I would finish high school in America. So, a host family was found to board and feed me and back I went. Destination, Lawton High School, Lawton, Oklahoma. Home of the Wolverines.

I wanted to be involved in all that I could and make the most of my newfound teenage freedom. So, I decided I needed to be a part of a group. Any group would do. First, I attempted to be a cheerleader. That ended in disastrous results. I won't go into great detail except to say that one cannot will one's self to do the Chinese splits. I should know. I tried and it simply cannot be done.

So, I turned my attention to the Highsteppers, the pom-pom squad comprised of about thirty girls who high-kicked their way to exhaustion on the football field every Friday night. The tryouts for this team were much easier. Grapevine left, grapevine right. Shuffle, shuffle. Kick, ball, change.

I made it, and although we were generally less popular than the cheerleaders, we had better outfits. We wore red satin skirts combined with red and white satin tops. We added white mid-calf boots and pristine white gloves. A white top hat completed our dramatic look. In addition to our pom-poms, we also used canes or hula-hoops from time to time. During football-game nights, we sat together in the bleachers. We admired the athletic prowess of the teenage Wolverines and gestured, waved, and clapped as we waited for our halftime performance. In short, things felt pretty good in high school. I was on the pom-pom team and had good grades. What else was there? Oh, I found out there was much more when a new girl came to town.

Her name was Becki. She was glamorous and mysterious. Rumor had it that she and her family had moved to Oklahoma from *Back East*. People said those two words with such reverence, almost in a whisper. *Back East*. She spoke with perfect diction and was the first girl I ever saw wear a three-piece pin-striped suit to school.

In addition to being from *Back East*, her family was also involved in politics on *Capitol Hill*. Yes, the same breathy whisper was used in reference to those two words, as well. *Capitol Hill*. To add to her sophistication, she took absolutely no interest in becoming a cheerleader or Highstepper. Instead, she wanted to run for class president and head up the debate team. I had very little knowledge about such things. However, I was introduced to the excitement of these subjects at an event called The Mock United Nations. I don't know if it is still occurring in high schools today, but back in the late '70s and early '80s, all students were required to take part in a three-day event that simulated what took place at the United Nations. There was a Security Council, and resolutions were submitted and passed or rejected. All of this took place in the high-school gymnasium. You could tell who the really intelligent students were. They were the ones hunkered down together, working like crazy on an environmental program or national security plan. They always represented the United States or the UK or some other really powerful country. Others of us just struggled to figure out what was going on and when lunch would be served. I was a delegate from Sweden. Not exactly a hotbed of political excitement.

While to this day I am still not exactly sure what I was supposed to learn from the three-day event, I can tell you what I observed. Becki held center court. She was Secretary General. Basically, in the world of the UN, she was the Big Dog. At the beginning of every session, she assembled her white index cards, walked to the podium, adjusted her pin-striped vest, and looked at the student body.

"Good morning, Delegates!" she said with such authority. She confidently adjusted the microphone at the same time. I believed that, in her mind, at that moment, she was Secretary General at the United Nations, not a high-school student in a stuffy gymnasium. She was also incredibly nice.

Shortly after we met, Becki invited me to her house for a party. And, not in the way that most high-schoolers invite other high-schoolers over. No, Becki's invitation was extended in true *Back East, Capitol Hill* fashion. It came by way of a creamy-white, embossed invitation that was delivered to my house by US Mail. I quickly RSVP'ed with an enthusiastic yes.

The night finally arrived. I worked diligently on my appearance and felt good about it. I wore a new smiley face tee shirt, Chic jeans, and Candie's shoes. I also managed to get my hair in a Farrah flip. When I knocked on her front door that night, I expected Becki to be dressed similarly. But when she opened the door, I was starstruck.

"WOW!" I exclaimed. "You look beautiful, Beck. What are you wearing?"

"Well, a hostess outfit, of course!" She smiled warmly. She twirled, the bright-fuchsia chiffon blouse floating around her. She had tucked the blouse into high-waist silk trousers. A sash was added with the bow perfectly positioned just over her left hip. On her feet she wore three-inch strappy sandals. Just then, her mother sidled up. She also wore a hostess outfit and was beautifully made up. She welcomed me and handed me a frothy, green drink.

"Thank you," I said. I looked at the drink. "What is this?"

"Well, a virgin margarita, of course!" She, too, smiled warmly. I had no idea what she meant, but I sipped the beverage anyway. I looked around the room. Beautiful leather furniture and softly lit lamps created an atmosphere of elegance. On the walls were pictures of The White House, the Washington Monument, the Chambers of the Senate and House, each illuminated with their own individual spotlight. People mingled everywhere. They sipped strange drinks and wore hostess outfits. No wonder people wanted to be from *Back East* and work on *Capitol Hill.*

The night was just lovely. Becki and her mother continued to serve exotic virgin drinks. They told amusing stories and then invited us all to their rec room. They turned on their television and what happened next was shocking. Truly shocking. Without warning, animation exploded onto the screen as we were taken on a Peter Pan flyby of some imaginary town. I was wide-eyed. I had never seen this show before! The music swelled as a huge voice boomed.

"This is HBO!!!!!"

"What is HBO?" I wondered. Count on cool, chic Becki to

be the first in the neighborhood to have HBO. I sat transfixed. There were no commercials, none at all. Just movie after movie for our enjoyment. The evening was filled with more virgin drinks, passed hors d'oeuvres, and commercial-free television. Man, what I was missing! High school was much more than just waving my pom-poms around. I wanted to be a part of this exotic world. First order of business: join the public-speaking team.

The very next year I had the opportunity to select my own electives. My guidance counselor looked at me oddly when I chose the public-speaking class. In all honesty, however, I had an ulterior motive. I had heard, through the grapevine, that the class was going to the National Mock UN in New York City later that year. I got into the class and was eager to be a part of my new world.

The class was taught by a teacher named Miss Wiggins. She was a kind, but firm teacher. Above all else, she wanted us to be ready for our performance in New York City. So we rehearsed relentlessly for the upcoming national mock UN. We practiced debating important issues, quizzed each other on parliamentary procedure, and brainstormed as to the resolutions we could put before the Security Council. Becki was the leader in our class. Always articulate, brilliant, and perfectly coiffed. In fact, the whole class was comprised of exceptionally intelligent people who generously ignored the fact that I had trouble just keeping my note cards arranged. Miss W gave me extra attention and help but I could tell she was a bit concerned.

Finally the day arrived for our class to travel to New York City for the National Mock United Nations. After we touched down at LaGuardia Airport, we made our way to an old, beautiful hotel that sat on a bustling street in the heart of midtown. We checked into our rooms and were told we needed to register immediately. Opening remarks were scheduled to begin that very afternoon. I went to the lobby and discovered that several long lines had already formed in front of temporary tables. High-school students from all across the country had gathered to begin the three-day session. I waited for my turn to register and listened as the official welcomed the girl in front of me.

"Welcome, Darla. You have been assigned to the Hungarian delegation. Please proceed to the grand mezzanine ballroom. You can take the center staircase or the elevator." Oh, that sounded quite exciting. "What's a grand mezzanine ballroom?" I wondered. No matter, I would soon find out. I was also eager to find out what country I had been assigned to. You see, several months prior to students arriving, their teachers had supplied their high-school record to the supervisors who ran the mock U.N. proceedings. Based on the student's level of debate experience and competitions, the officials determined where the student would be assigned for the three days. I could only imagine how pitiful my sheet of credentials must have looked to the organizers.

"Hello, I'm Lisa Mason from Lawton High School in Lawton, Oklahoma. Checking in," I said with a dazzling smile. The receptionist looked down at her sheet and searched for my name. I couldn't wait to discover the wonders of a grand mezzanine ballroom. I hoped desperately that I was part of a super-cool delegation.

"Oh, yes, I see you here," the registrar said. I held my breath and waited for my assignment.

"Yes, yes. You will be part of the auxiliary group," she said. "Please report to room D-2 down that hallway." She pointed down the hall where the bathrooms were located. She gave me a sticky nametag with my name and the word "auxiliary" printed on it.

"You will need to put this on your dress," she said. I mumbled something as I slapped the nametag on my chest. I didn't care if it was crooked or not.

I walked down the hall to D-2 but then changed course and made my way to the grand staircase. With all of the bustling high-school students, I joined the crowd unnoticed. I was determined to see what a grand mezzanine ballroom looked like.

Up the stairs, a beautiful landing greeted me. Cherry wood walls were polished to a high finish, the carpet beneath my feet felt like clouds. Bountiful flower arrangements complemented the side tables and soft music filled the air. I walked with the crowd toward the grand mezzanine ballroom entrance. What a vision. I peered in and saw tables covered with white tablecloths. The chandeliers suspended from the ceiling were softly lit and created a glowing atmosphere. Everywhere were serving carts with silver-plated water pitchers, crystal glasses, coffee urns, and cream and sugar containers. The hotel workers scurried around and laid out napkins and flatware so that the delegates could easily stir their coffee without their thoughts being interrupted.

I walked further inside. Across the ballroom, I saw Becki. Sheer perfection in a three-piece suit, she was at the United States table. As head of the delegation, she made notes and talked with great animation. How impressive! This was where I wanted to be. My mind raced with ideas as to how I could get a seat in the ballroom. Perhaps if I took off the nametag. I attempted to peel it off, but it tore and left telltale bits of glue on my dress. I looked around to see if I could steal someone else's nametag. Anything except being exiled to the auxiliary room. But, before I could come up with a plan, one of the chaperons who patrolled the room looked at my nametag.

"Oh, hello, uh, Lisa," she said, as she read my nametag, "I know you probably want to stay for opening remarks, but we just don't have enough seats. It would probably be best if you went to your room. You will be more comfortable there, OK?" she said. I looked at her sadly and hesitated.

"Why don't I show you where your room is!" she said. She sensed my reluctance. I despondently left the grand mezzanine ballroom heaven I had just discovered. I followed the teacher back down the center staircase and down the hallway that housed the bathrooms, the laundry room, and the room known as D-2, the auxiliary room.

"Here we are," she said. "I will introduce you to everyone." Evidently, she had already made one or two trips.

"Lisa, this is Tina and Rory." She pointed out the two people in the room.

"Hi," I said. The small room was illuminated with harsh fluorescent lights and outfitted with metal folding chairs and a card table. In the corner, a water cooler gurgled. Where were the beautiful tablecloths, the soft music, the elegant chandeliers?

Tina looked up from the paperback novel she was reading. She had braided tiny jingle bells into her long brown hair. They made a slight tinkling noise when she waved. Rory had black fuzzy hair and wore black-rimmed, thick glasses. He looked at me with a scowl and said nothing.

"Well," said the teacher, "someone will be along in a while to get you started with your resolution." She left. Tina, Rory, and I looked at each other. I went over to the water fountain and got a drink. Next door, the industrial-strength washers went into motion, the sloshing sound of wet towels and bed linens filled our room. Tina read, Rory looked angry, and I drank water.

After about an hour of waiting, a teacher popped into our room and said we were excused for the rest of the day. She said we should report back to D-2 the following morning at 9:30 a.m. I, of course, did not report back to D-2 the following morning; I did, however, discover the wonders of walking the streets of New York City.

Once back at Lawton high, I quit the public-speaking team. I decided that being a pom-pom girl wasn't so bad after all. Try as I might, I didn't fit into Becki's *Back East, Capitol Hill* world. So, I just stayed in my own.

****

Fitting in. That universally understood desire to be accepted. Sometimes, harmless, as in my experience at Lawton High School. But sometimes, not so harmless.

Over the years, I have watched countless friends risk anything and everything to fit in. I have witnessed them augment themselves to such a degree that they were barely recognizable afterward. And for what? To fit into the mold of someone else's image of perfection or acceptability? Because, as it turns out, you **can** put a square peg in a round hole. All you have to do is hack off the edges, whittle down the sides, and sand off the rough spots. And, there you are. Round. But for me, I prefer to stay square. That way I can grapevine left, grapevine right, shuffle, shuffle, kick-ball-change for the rest of my life.

Big Life Lesson Number Three: 'Fitting in' is pretty great. Realizing that you don't need to is even better.

FOUR:

Living With Regret.

A "do-over." That opportunity to attempt something a second time after royally screwing it up the first time around. I know a thing or two about do-overs. I had them often during elementary school and usually during T-ball. I recall clearly: I would enter the batter's area with great determination and choke up on the giant, plastic bat as my daddy taught me. I would bend my knees and squint hard at the huge, white ball positioned right in front of me. After a count of three, I would swing with all my might. But the sound of *whoosh* that followed my swing indicated that my bat had made contact only with air. Without hesitation, however, I would scream, "DO-OVER!" at the top of my lungs. I would choke up, bend my knees, squint, count, and swing again. In second-grade T-ball, you could have as many do-overs as you wanted. No harm, no foul, no penalty.

If only life were that easy.

****

As you already know, I attended Lawton High School in Oklahoma. From there, I moved to Stillwater, Oklahoma, to attend Oklahoma State University. My plan was to finish a four-year degree and find a job. But, it didn't exactly work out that way. I flunked out. Really flunked out.

I soon realized that my best course of action was to leave Stillwater, where the jobs were scarce, and move to a bigger town with the hopes of finding work. I had depleted my funds while at OSU and would have to find a way to save some money before I enrolled in another university. Of course, I would also have to find a college that would accept my crummy transcript, but that would come later. I decided that Oklahoma City sounded like a good place to move, so off I went. First order of business was to find a place to live so that I could look for employment. That's where she came in. I will call her Mary, although that is not her real name. I don't have the right to call her by name. You will find out why later.

I moved into her apartment in the summer. In actuality, it was an old two-story house that had been converted into four apartments. Each apartment had two bedrooms, one bathroom, a kitchen, a living area, and a small dining area. Her apartment was on the second floor, up a steep flight of stairs. She had lived there for several years and had claimed the larger of the two bedrooms. She offered to move to the smaller one so that I could have the larger one, but since I could barely afford the rent as it was, I took the smaller one on the opposite end of the apartment, just off the living room.

At first, things went fine. I worked as a waitress in a seafood restaurant. My shift was four o'clock in the afternoon till midnight. She worked as a secretary at a local business. She left in the morning at seven o'clock, long before I dragged myself out of bed. She didn't get home until after I left for work in the afternoons so, frankly, our paths didn't cross that often. Sometimes, we found ourselves at home together. We occasionally ate takeout or watched a movie, but mostly I went out with other people and left her there alone. Once, I invited her to go out with my friends, but she acted so strangely that I didn't ask her again. This schedule went on for several months. We saw each other infrequently, two ships that just passed in the night, as they say. I liked it because nothing was required of me except a rent check on the fifteenth of each month. But then, everything changed.

She lost her job. She was informed that her company had downsized and they didn't need her anymore. She got a very small severance, just enough to keep her going for a few months. She immediately started looking for work. I would come in from the restaurant around one o'clock in the morning and see her at the small dining room table, hunched over the classifieds. She read and circled ads, lost in her own thoughts. As she read, she pulled her hair. She twirled the ends of her brunette hair around her pointer finger and yanked with all her might. With each motion, her shoulder blades protruded through her thin tee shirt. She was impossibly skinny. Once, I noticed that she read the same ads over and over again. I almost asked her about it, but I didn't. It wasn't any of my business. Her job search continued and, as it did, I became more and more uncomfortable in her presence. She was a different person each day. Sometimes, she talked up a blue streak and sometimes she barely uttered more than a word. I found as many reasons as possible to stay out of the apartment. But, eventually, the weather turned cold and I was forced to stay at home.

It was January. She had left the apartment for a job interview one day. I was off that morning so I decided to do some housework. And, it was desperately needed. When I first moved into her apartment, I was impressed with how clean she kept the place. The kitchen and bathroom were spotless and the living room furniture was polished to a high shine. But, after she lost her job, it all changed. The kitchen stank and the bathroom stank. Literally reeked. So did her bedroom, probably from the overflowing laundry basket. We didn't have a washer or dryer, so we loaded up our clothes once a week and schlepped them to a local laundromat. My waitressing clothes sometimes smelled so strongly of fried food that I had to go more frequently, sometimes every other day. But, by the looks of her room, when I peeked in, it was obvious that she had not been to the laundromat in at least two weeks.

I went into the kitchen. There was clutter everywhere. Refrigerated items were out on the counter, plates with several-days-old food were on the table. I rarely went into the kitchen and I never cooked, since my meals came from the restaurant or from a drive-through. The most I did was make the occasional pot of coffee. So, I started my task with extreme frustration since this wasn't my mess to begin with.

I looked around to see what needed my attention first. I decided it was the pots and pans in the sink. They had been "soaking" there for at least a week. I suspected they were the culprit of the stench in the room. I took them out of the sink and carefully dumped the greasy water back in. I placed them on the counter. I cringed as I plunged my hand into the icy water. I felt around on the bottom of the sink, trying to find the plug. When my fingers touched something fleshy, I recoiled. I truly hated her at that moment.

I finally found the drain plug and pulled hard. The water gurgled slowly away. On the bottom of the sink was what looked like large pieces of fried hamburger meat, but after several days of sitting in water, they had turned spongy and gray. I reached for paper towels. I knew I needed to make several trips to the trash can to get rid of all the rotten meat in the sink. I took several sheets from the roll and scooped out as much as I could. The smell was horrific. As I walked to the trash can on the other side of the kitchen, I noticed that the lid was on. I knew it required both of my hands to pry the large lid off, so I put the wad of paper towels back on the counter. I pulled the trash can lid off and was about to throw the paper towels away, when something caught my eye. Just beneath several sheets of crumpled-up classified pages was a plastic bag. In that bag were lots of small boxes. I reached in and pulled the whole thing out. I opened it and looked inside. Ex-lax, at least thirty boxes. All empty. Well, that certainly explained the smell coming from the bathroom. I stood for a minute and wondered what to do. Should I say something to her? Was it my business? She wasn't really a friend. She was just someone I rented a room from, so I decided to think about it later. I finished cleaning the kitchen.

I went to work that evening and didn't see her until the next day. She had cleaned her room and the bathroom. She had stocked the refrigerator. She had found money from somewhere, obviously. I didn't ask her about it but I assumed she had found a new job. So it went. We went back to our old routine. I, gone all night. She, gone all day. But then another change occurred and this time it was because of my job.

From the very beginning, I worked the evening shift at the restaurant. I preferred to cater to the dinner crowd. The bill for the evening meal was higher and, as a result, the tips were better. But, sales in the evening had slowed down so the owner of our restaurant decided to serve lunch only to see if he could improve the profit margin. I didn't like the change, but I didn't have a choice. I needed to work. I hadn't seen Mary in a few days, so I hadn't had a chance to inform her of my new schedule, but I knew I would run into her eventually, so I wasn't concerned.

On the first day of my new schedule, I arrived at work around ten o'clock in the morning. I did prep work and worked the lunch crowd. When the restaurant closed at four o'clock, I cleaned the tables, refilled the salt and pepper shakers, sorted silverware, and swept the floors. Afterward, I sat down and counted my tips. Other waiters and waitresses did the same, as was our ritual. We nibbled on food and laughed for a while. I left the restaurant at about six o'clock, but didn't head for home.

I had loaded my car with my dirty clothes earlier that morning with the intention of going to the laundromat immediately after work. I considered blowing the whole thing off, but knew I would regret it later. So, off to the laundromat I went. It was crowded. It seemed that early evening was prime time for clothes to be washed. Finally, a washer was available. I stuffed whites and coloreds in together. I didn't care. I waited for the wash to be completed and pulled my clothes out and placed them into a rolling basket. I looked around. All the dryers were taken. I sat down and read an ancient issue of *Good Housekeeping* magazine to pass the time. Finally, a dryer was free. By the time it was all said and done, I didn't get back to the apartment until ten o'clock that night. I was hot and ill tempered. I knew I had to get up early the next morning and do the lunch shift again. I realized I had to find a new job.

I climbed the staircase to our apartment, laundry basket in tow. I stepped onto the landing and reached for my front door key. I opened the door and went inside. All the lights were off. It was pitch black. I found the wall switch and turned on the overhead light, confused. It seemed that Mary was out. I walked toward my bedroom and intended to put my clean clothes away when I heard music. It came from her bedroom on the opposite end of the apartment.

"Well," I thought, "she is home. But, why are all the lights off?" I wondered. I put my laundry basket on the floor and walked down the hallway toward her bedroom. The door was shut. There was no light shining from under her door. "Is she sitting in the dark all alone?" I wondered. I was concerned and decided to check in on her. I lifted my hand to knock when I heard a voice. Hers. Then, a man's voice. And then, a different man's voice. There were two men in her bedroom. I stood for a moment and listened until I was sure of what was going on. Then, I turned and walked back down the hallway. I got my laundry basket and went into my room. I put my clothes away and shut the door. I waited.

Mary's guests prepared to leave at about midnight or so. I listened as the two men walked through the apartment and laughed. I smelled pot. They were in the living room, just off my bedroom. Mary told them it was time for them to go. She said her roommate would be getting home soon. Remember, she still thought that I worked the evening shift.

"Thanks for the party, babe," one of the men said. I heard the shuffle of footsteps as someone walked toward the front door.

"Aren't you forgetting something?" she asked.

"We'll catch you next time," he said. More footsteps. The other man must have also walked toward the front door. They both laughed.

"Hey, that's not what we agreed to," she said, her voice quivered.

"Too bad," he said. "Let's get out of here, man," he said to his friend. They laughed. The front door slammed. They left.

I heard the scrape of the dining room chair as it was pulled out from the table. I heard the rattle of newspaper. I opened my door. There she was, hunched over the classifieds. She twirled and pulled her hair with all her strength. It was a second or two before she looked up. Her eyes widened. She realized that I had not come in from the front door, but from my bedroom. I had been there all along. I knew everything. She started to say something.

I held up my hand and said, "It's none of my business." I walked back into my bedroom and closed the door. Thus, began my silent treatment.

Now that I am older, I understand how unfair the silent treatment is. When you ignore a person, you make them feel worthless or, worse, invisible. You close down all aspects of communication so they can't explain their side of the story. But, I wasn't grown up then. And, I wasn't the least bit compassionate. I wanted nothing to do with her, nothing to do with her depression, mood swings, laxatives, pot smoking, or her promiscuity. I thought that if I acknowledged her, I would be filthy by association.

The next morning I left the apartment as early as possible. I went to the restaurant and worked the lunch shift. At the end of my workday, I asked my coworkers if they knew of anyone who had a room I could rent. They said that they didn't know of anyone but would ask around. I left work and went to a movie with one of my fellow waitresses. After the movie, we went out for coffee. I got home around ten p.m. and went straight to my room. I avoided her at all costs.

Over the next couple of days, she left little notes on my door asking if we could talk. I threw them away. I made sure I put them in one of the wastebaskets that she used so that she could see them. I left early each morning and got home late each night. I could not wait to move out. In fact, I boxed my things up in hopes that someone from work would give me a place to crash. This went on for about a week and then, one early morning, I knew I had to go. I awoke to the squeaking sound the living-room floor made when someone tiptoed on it. I got out of bed and cracked open my bedroom door. All I got was a brief glimpse as she and a new companion walked down the hallway, toward her bedroom. Enough, I decided.

The next morning, I left for good. My rent was paid up for the month, so I didn't leave her in a lurch. I almost left a note, but decided against it. She knew how I felt about her. I loaded up my car with my belongings and went to the restaurant. I worked the lunch shift as usual. Afterward, I drove around until I found an extended-stay, budget hotel. I couldn't afford it, but I did it anyway. It was such a relief to be out of the apartment and away from Mary. And so it went. I eventually found a new roommate and moved out of the hotel. I worked and saved and finally returned to school. I didn't think about Mary again for a long time.

Three years passed. I finished my junior year at college and worked as a part-time receptionist at a fund-raising office. It wasn't exciting work, but I only had to do it a couple of hours a day. I got to know a couple of girls in the office and, as improbable as it seems, I discovered that one of them actually grew up in the same town as Mary. I don't remember how the conversation started, but somehow we realized that her childhood friend named Mary and the Mary I once lived with was the same person. I asked her if she talked to Mary. She said she didn't; in fact, she hadn't laid eyes on Mary in years. She kept in touch sporadically, she said, but only by mail. But, she wasn't surprised, given Mary's situation.

She explained that, from the very beginning, the cards were stacked against Mary. She was raised in a tiny town by very conservative parents. They homeschooled her and rarely allowed her to leave the house. They were strict disciplinarians and punished her for the slightest infraction. The only place

Mary was allowed to go was church. That was where Mary met my coworker.

"She must have been lonely," I said.

"Not always," she said.

"Why?" I asked.

"Because of her sister," she said. She recounted the story of Julie, known as "Julie, the beautiful" around the small community. Tall, brunette, and gorgeous, she was fourteen years older than Mary. She left home when Mary was around six years of age or so, but she had been in Mary's life long enough to make a big impression. When Mary was in her room, alone, having been punished for yet another mistake, it was the thought of Julie that kept Mary going. Though Julie never came home for a visit, Mary sustained herself with fantasies that Julie would someday take her away. She dreamed that the two of them would live together. As her real world disintegrated, her fantasy world took over. Mary convinced herself that her sister not only actually lived in a big city but she was also a successful model. Over time, she believed it so much that she started to talk about it to her friends at church.

"I don't know," my coworker continued, "I think we were about twelve years old when it happened. We were at a church function. And, there was Mary, bragging once again about her sister and how famous she was and how she was coming home to take her away."

"What happened?" I asked.

"One of the girls, I don't remember who, finally just said out loud what we all knew," she replied.

"You mean, that Mary was making it all up and that her sister wasn't really a model and wasn't really coming back to rescue her?" I laughed.

"Was this the big painful secret in her life?" I thought.

"That she had an overactive imagination? Big deal."

"Well, not exactly," my coworker said, "actually, what she said was that Mary's sister was never coming back because…," she hesitated. I could tell she was deciding if she should continue the story or not.

"Because why?" I pressed her.

"Because Mary's sister," she whispered, "was also her mother." I looked at her. I did not understand what she was talking about.

"What?" I said. "I don't get what you are saying."

"Her sister was also her mother," she repeated.

"I don't understand," I said. "How could her sister also be her mother?" I asked stupidly.

"Her sister gave birth to her," she said, slowly, patiently. I still didn't get it.

"But if Mary's sister was also her mother," I said, "then who was her father?" I asked.

"Her father," she said.

"No, no," I said, "who was Mary's biological father?"

"Her father," she repeated, sadly.

"Do you mean….?" my question trailed off as I thought about what she had just said. I finally got it.

"Oh," I said and looked at the floor. I had never talked about incest. I guess on some conscious level I knew about it, but I didn't think it really happened. I never imagined that it actually occurred to ordinary, everyday people. But, I guess it did.

"Mary never knew?" I asked, finally.

"Not until that day at church," she said. "From what I understand, she confronted her parents after that church function. Oh, they denied it. But, we all knew. I mean, the whole town knew about it."

"Why didn't someone tell her? Why didn't someone try to

protect her?" I asked, incredulous.

"I guess people felt it was none of their business," she answered. A familiar refrain.

"What happened after that?" I asked.

"I guess things went back to normal," she said. "Her family continued to attend church. They homeschooled her. I mean, she was more quiet and she never talked about her sister again, but I guess it all turned out all right." She paused, then continued. "Although, there was more talk about Mary, but it never amounted to much."

"What talk?" I asked.

"Well," she said, "people in town figured that if it happened once, it would happen again. When she was about fourteen or so, it looked like she was getting big in the belly, but then it suddenly went away. She never had a baby, so I guess it never happened."

"Oh," I said for the second time. I looked again at the floor. I reeled from the full extent of the story. I could only imagine the pain of Mary's life. Forced to attend a church and go out into the community amid stares and silent accusations.

"That's why I was so glad she finally got out of that crappy little town," my coworker said, "so glad she connected with nice people. So glad she finally had friends, like you." She looked at me with an expression of such sincerity. Her words held no malice. She meant it. "Thank God she got a second chance at life," she continued.

"Yes," I said, "thank God."

"Do the two of you stay in touch?" she asked.

"Well, uh, no." I stumbled on my words. "We lost track of each other," I said quietly, a convenient lie.

"Oh," she replied, a look of disappointment on her face, "that's a shame."

"Yes," I said, "it is a shame."

A shame.

A shame I will live with for the rest of my life.

Mary was punished at birth for a sin she never committed. Held accountable for something she could never change. As a child, she tried to save herself by creating a safe haven in her imagination, but soon, it too was destroyed, ripped away in the most cruel fashion. She desired that the silence be broken so that she could put an end to the allegations, rumors, and speculations. But on it went. As a teenager, she went through a normal growing spurt. But, her community assumed the very worst. When she finally broke free, she wanted only peace. She asked for nothing, only gave. But, when her luck once again ran out, her mind turned dark, and with it came a physical need to purge the horrid past from her body. And, when she was forced to find money in whatever way she could, she was met with ridicule, sanctimonious judgment, and, finally, silence. She was invisible, all over again.

And this time, I did it.

****

When I was little, my daddy told me that life was a bit like playing ball. Some people start their lives with every advantage in the book, he said. Good parents, a nice home, and a friendly community. Kind of like being the first at bat during a game of T-ball. You have all your outs and the ball is positioned right in front of you, stationary, ready for your swing. You can't lose.

But other people, he said, start life very differently. They find themselves in a game of fast-pitch baseball. They have no support, no coach, and no experience. They go to bat with two outs and no one on the bases. No one believes in them. They don't have a chance. I asked him what should be done. He said it was very simple. He said the lucky T-ball person should walk over to the unlucky baseball person and take them by the hand.

"Then what?" I asked.

"Well, the lucky T-ball person should give the unlucky baseball person their place at bat."

"Why?" I asked.

"So that the unlucky baseball person could finally hit one out of the park, prove all those people wrong," he said. If only I had listened more closely to my daddy.

I don't know where Mary is. I searched for her but came up with nothing. Honestly, I don't know what I would say to her if I found her, anyway.

The lessons that I learned from this experience are numerous. Too numerous to recount. But, the one I think is the most important is this: sometimes, forgiveness is not immediately possible. Don't misunderstand. I believe that God has forgiven me for my behavior. No, the forgiveness I seek is my own, and I just can't give it. At least, not yet.

Big Life Lesson Number Four: There is no pain like the pain of regret.

FIVE:

Winning Contests.

For most of my life, I believed there were two distinctively different types of people in this world. Those who always seemed to win and those who rarely seemed to win. I fell into the latter category. I rarely won. In fact, I can only think of one time that I actually won something.

****

I lived in Oklahoma City. You probably remember that after my less-than-stellar performance at Oklahoma State University, I moved to Oklahoma City in an attempt to save money and get back into school. I worked several years as a waitress and one year at a fund-raising office. Finally, I saved enough and was accepted to the University of Central Oklahoma, just outside of Oklahoma City. There, I finished my Bachelor of Arts degree with an emphasis on news broadcasting. I sent my résumé out and, fortunately, landed a job. And, not just any job, but the one I really wanted.

I sought employment at one of the nation's most respected PBS affiliates. I wanted more than anything to work for OETA, partially because it was affiliated with PBS but mostly because of the reputation of the station manager, Mr. Thrash. In

Oklahoma and the surrounding states, he was known as the man who knew something about everything. He could spout off dates and names of practically every important event that had ever occurred in Oklahoma. Add to that the fact that he was soft-spoken, fair-minded, patient, and a regular contributor to the arts. And don't think for a moment that he didn't have opportunities to go to other states. He was regularly recruited for much higher-profile jobs but instead chose to stay in his beloved state of Oklahoma.

Several months after I got the job as a news reporter, Mr. Thrash generously offered to set up an interview for me with Mary Hart. Yes, that Mary Hart. You see, they had a great friendship. Mary worked with Mr. Thrash in Oklahoma City years earlier and the two had remained close friends even after her move to California and *Entertainment Tonight*. Since I was new to the business, Mr. Thrash suggested that we prepare the questions together. He patiently went over everything with me and arranged for the interview location. The day was upon us. I felt very confident. OK, overconfident. Don't ask me why, but on the day of the interview I decided to stray away from the questions we rehearsed and try some of my own. What a mistake. For the record, Mary Hart was gracious and lovely. She listened and smiled and probably just tried to make sense of my ridiculous questions. In addition, I had decided to dress in all white for the interview. White shoes, hose, skirt, jacket and, to complete my look, white pearl earrings. What was I thinking? Did I think that it made me look angelic? Had I completely lost my mind?

Several days after the interview, Mr. Thrash invited me to review the program with him. It was scheduled to air later that month and I had not yet seen it. We watched. I was mortified. My questions were sophomoric, I acted slightly arrogant, and my outfit made me look like Casper the Friendly Ghost. "Well, this is it," I thought to myself, "I am certainly going to be fired. Not only had I done a poor job professionally, but I had also probably embarrassed Mr. Thrash in front of his friend." At the conclusion of the horrific interview, Mr. Thrash turned off the tape and looked at me. He was silent for a moment. I held my breath.

"Well," he said, "how do you think your interview went?"

I was silent for a moment, so humbled by this question. He graciously gave me the chance to talk first when he could have launched into a laundry list of all my missteps. I took a deep breath and listed all of my obvious mistakes and all of my missed opportunities. I expressed regret in the way that I had handled what should have been a very successful experience. Mr. Thrash nodded and smiled, made a few more recommendations for future interviews, and ended the meeting.

Time passed. I worked very hard to improve. I wanted to be a good and responsible reporter and make Mr. Thrash proud. Then, after several years, I felt I was ready to take on a new challenge. You see, I had written and produced long-form stories for a while and enjoyed the process of researching and investigating a subject at great length. And, while I had covered several serious topics, none of them were as serious as the one I proposed to Mr. Thrash.

"It will be called *Faces of AIDS*," I said to him. "It will be about people in our state who are living with HIV." He looked at me. By his expression, I could tell he was thinking about it, but was concerned. You see, this was almost two decades ago, a time before true understanding existed about the disease. You may not remember this, but in the early '90s, people thought AIDS could be spread by simply being in the same room with an HIV-positive person; they thought you could get infected by just breathing the same air. It was a time of extreme prejudice. But, after some consideration, Mr. Thrash finally agreed. And so, it began. I fortunately found people who allowed me into their lives. People who let me into their homes for hours at a time to tell their story. My intent was to show that all sorts of people get the disease in many different ways. I wanted to show that HIV was in every community, not just the gay community. And while all the stories were compelling, one was extra special to me. It revolved around a little girl.

Her name was Lacy. She was two years old when I met her. She was one of the most beautiful children I had ever laid eyes on. Her skin was like porcelain, her eyes sky-blue. When I first saw her, she had already been diagnosed. She had developed pneumonia early that summer. Her parents had taken her to the children's hospital. The physicians never suspected HIV, so they never tested her. They treated her for the pneumonia and briefly she got better. She returned home with her parents but, eventually, she got sick again and returned to the hospital. It was after several more trips to the emergency room that one of the doctors finally decided to test her for HIV. It was a long shot, but the physicians had run out of ideas as to why she was so ill. That was the last option. So, they did the test.

When I held her for the first time, she was like a rag doll. She lay limply in my arms, her feeding tube protruding from her abdomen. She rarely opened her eyes, but when she did, they were glassy. I thought that it was very wrong for such a small baby to be so heavily medicated. Her tiny body gave off a nauseatingly sweet odor. I learned later that the human body produces that smell when it is in the process of dying.

All of this was told in my news story. But there was more. You see, the doctors had to find out why Lacy was infected with HIV in the first place. So they interviewed her parents about possible blood transfusions, accidents, anything that would explain her condition. When nothing was discovered, the doctors finally agreed that Lacy's mother had to be tested. Perhaps she had somehow passed the disease on to Lacy during childbirth. Lacy's mother agreed, confident that the test would come back negative, but eager to do anything to get to the bottom of the mystery. Back then, test results sometimes took as long as a week to get. The wait was agonizing for Lacy's parents. By that time, Lacy was gravely ill. So sick, in fact, that she was permanently placed in the hospital. And so, it was there, in the hospital, at Lacy's bedside, that her mother got the results. She, too, was HIV-positive. She told me about that day in the hospital. The shame and the confusion. She didn't understand how she had contracted the disease or when. She didn't understand any of it. The doctors, thankfully, gave the parents a couple of days to get over the latest shock before they made yet another request. Lacy's father had to be tested, also. It was almost too much to bear. The agonizing wait, the fear. Then, the results. Yes, he was also infected. The doctors were additionally concerned because both adults had been HIV-positive for so long with no treatment. They feared that their disease had progressed past the point of no return.

In my story, I focused on Lacy's parents and how incredible they were. They spoke openly about their daughter and their love for her. They also spoke about their own HIV-positive diagnosis. However, they never were able to pinpoint just how it all started. Did he give it to her? Did she give it to him? They didn't care. All they cared about was staying alive long enough to properly bury their precious child.

Faces of AIDS aired on PBS on April 15, 1993. Shortly after that, it was nominated for an Emmy award. Shortly after that, Lacy died. Her parents called me and told me. Although our work together had long since been completed, they still allowed me into their lives. They asked me if I would attend the funeral. I told them I would. They had experienced great difficulty in finding a church that would allow them to have a service. It seemed that many churches felt that their HIV infection would somehow contaminate the sanctuary. But, finally, one was found.

It was a massive church on the far side of town. It was not one that represented their faith, but they had no choice. They wanted their daughter to have a church funeral. I arrived and entered the building. At first, I thought I was in the wrong place. No one seemed to be there. But, I walked down the aisle and noticed a couple of people sitting on the front row. It was the right place, after all. The coffin was tiny and pink and required only one person to carry it. The service was brief. I embraced them both as I left.

She, wafer-thin from her illness, whispered in my ear, "We made it."

"You sure did." I whispered back. I looked at her and smiled. I understood. They had succeeded in their last parental task. They had both held on long enough to bury their child.

That fall, I flew out west to attend the Emmy Awards. It was an incredible experience, one I will never forget. The ballroom was filled to capacity and cameras clicked as celebrities arrived. Our Master of Ceremonies was Stone Phillips, his deep, rich voice boomed through the auditorium.

When he got to my category, I could barely breathe. When *Faces of AIDS* was called as the winner, I could barely move. My sister, Amanda, had come with me. She nudged me and told me to go up! I had won. I had won. I walked up onto the stage and to the podium. I accepted my statuette and thanked all the appropriate people. I attended the party that followed that evening with my sister. The next morning, we flew home, Emmy in hand.

Shortly after that, Lacy's parents died. So did all the other people I profiled in my documentary. The following year, I left OETA. I felt I had completed my work there. I packed up and moved away. I took my award with me.

Without fail, when friends come to visit, it is the first thing they would want to see and hold. To them, I am sure it is beautiful, shaped as an angel with wings stretched upward. The plaque on the bottom bears my name and the name of the documentary. It is quite impressive. But, to me, it only represents the loss of an innocent child.

****

For most of my life, I believed that there were two distinctively different types of people in this world. Those who always seemed to win and those who rarely seemed to win. I fell into the latter category. In fact, I only won something once in my life. And, interestingly, it left me feeling empty. That's when I realized that winning has nothing to do with riding in parades or accepting awards. It has nothing to do with ribbons, medals, or trophies, those items that collect in our curio cabinets to be taken out from time to time to prove our achievements.

No, real winning has to do with facing each day as it comes and dealing with whatever life dishes out. And I suspect that real winners move among us each day, every day. We just don't see them. Real winners are people like Lacy's parents who put aside their private agony to focus solely on their child, until the very end.

I used to believe that there were two distinctively different types of people in this world. Now, I understand that there are three. Those who always seem to win. Those who rarely seem to win. And those who are the wisest. They are the ones who don't have the slightest interest in entering frivolous, earthly contests in the first place. Because they know that their greatest reward is in the future. It is in Heaven. And it is waiting for them.

Big Life Lesson Number Five: Know which contests are truly worth winning.

SIX:

Being A Lifeline.

What is a lifeline? *Webster's Dictionary* defines it like this: 1. A rope or line thrown to rescue someone in difficulties. 2. A thing that is essential for the continued existence of someone or something which provides a means of escape.

Lifelines can take on many forms. And they can come when you least expect them but need them the most.

****

I parked my Nissan Sentra in the QVC parking lot and yawned loudly. I was so tired. I folded down the sun visor and looked at my appearance in the lighted mirror.

"Good Lord," I said in disgust. The past several months had certainly taken their toll. My face looked bloated and blotchy. My hair, growing out from a bad haircut, was matted down. Several months earlier I had taken a picture to my stylist, but try as she might, she just couldn't duplicate the look. The end result was something along the lines of a female mullet. Yep, Billy Ray Cyrus and I certainly had something in common.

I put a baseball cap on my mullet-head and reached over to the passenger-side seat to grab my garment bag. I wasn't on the air until 4:00 a.m., so I had plenty of time to change my clothes before my shift. I wore big, baggy sweatpants and a sweatshirt. Partly because they were comfy and warm in the chilly spring air. Partly because they hid the ten pounds I had recently put on.

I opened the door of the car and got out. I yawned loudly again as I walked across the dark parking lot toward the building, my thoughts replaying the past three months.

I had just moved to Philadelphia. Before that, I lived in Oklahoma City and worked at the Public Television station as a news anchor. A small station, it was made up of wonderful people who became close friends. I loved it, just as I loved Oklahoma. But a position at an electronic retailing network became available and I was ready for something new. So, three months ago, I took the job at QVC, and realized immediately that I had made a mistake.

You see, this new job was about selling items on television. Learning about products and then presenting those items with the sole intention of getting viewers to buy them. I was trained in reporting news stories, not selling products. Don't get me wrong. The training and support from QVC was professional and very thorough. It's just that I didn't belong. Add to that, the schedule was brutal. Every new host was required to work what is known as the "overnight" shift. Generally, that meant that the host was on the air between the hours of 1:00 a.m. and 6:00 a.m. I tried to adjust to the schedule but found it very difficult. I hated my new life.

Just then, a car entered the parking lot. Its bright headlights startled me out of my thoughts. I shifted my garment bag to the other arm and opened the front door to the lobby. I said hello to security and walked down the long hallway to the host lounge. I intended to drop my things and prepare for my shift.

It was then that I noticed a group of people walking toward

me. I didn't have my contact lenses in, so I squinted to see who it was. I made out about five or six people. They chatted and laughed and vied for the attention of the person who walked in the middle of the group. I continued my pace as did the group. I squinted a bit harder and finally made out who was coming toward me. Joan Rivers. The Joan Rivers. Good Lord, I looked like something the cat dragged up. I frantically searched for a doorway I could duck into, a bathroom, anything. There was nothing. The group came closer and closer. I quickly realized I would have to introduce myself. After all, I was a host and eventually I would work with Ms. Rivers.

Finally, we were close enough for me to speak. Her group stopped as I said hello.

"Well, hello," she said.

"I just wanted to introduce myself to you!" I said to her, my heart pounded through my chest.

I extended my hand. "I am a new host," I sputtered, "my name is..." My mind went completely blank.

"Joan!" I barked. Sweet Lord, the humiliation. "I mean, I'm not Joan. You're Joan. That's you!" I felt my face turn beet red. "I'm Lisa." I continued on.

"It is very nice to meet you," she said. She extended her hand to me. "I look forward to working with you," she continued, obviously embarrassed for me. I stared at her as we shook hands. I couldn't think of a thing to say. I scrambled for anything.

"I love your necklace!" I blurted out. My face turned even more crimson.

"Well, thank you," she said. "Have a good night." Her group walked toward the exit. I raced to the host lounge. I prayed that the floor would swallow me up. Later, I told my husband Gino about the incident. He said it was kind of funny when you thought about it. I told him that I didn't see the humor. So, he changed the subject and asked me about the business trip that I was about to take.

You see, QVC was in the midst of a broadcasting tour, of sorts. Each week, the network broadcast live from a different state. The tour had been going on for a while and, as a rule, only senior hosts were invited to go on the trip. But, since the very next state that was to be visited was Oklahoma, and since I had just moved from there, the management of QVC felt that I should host the show. In fact, I was traveling alone, one day ahead of the crew, to do preliminary work for the show. So, the very next week, off I went.

****

The flight attendant finished her instructions for takeoff. She reminded passengers about tray tables, oxygen masks, and emergency exits. I glanced briefly around the half-empty plane. Most people slept, a few read, but no one seemed to be paying attention. If she noticed, the attendant didn't appear to mind.

My eyes felt heavy. I glanced at my watch. We were scheduled for a 6:38 a.m. departure and it looked as if we would leave on time. I had been assigned to the window seat, row fourteen. When I had boarded the jet several minutes earlier, I had prayed that the seat next to me would remain empty so that I might sleep during the flight. Luck had been with me. No one had been assigned as my seatmate.

Directly across the aisle, a businessman pulled a *Wall Street Journal* from his briefcase. He opened it and snapped it into place, the pages made a crackling sound as he turned them. In the row in front of him, an elderly couple settled in for the journey. The woman reminded the man that he needed to take his medication. He argued that he felt fine.

I looked out the window. The morning sky was gray, heavy.

"Good morning, ladies and gentlemen," a man's voice boomed over the PA system, "this is your captain speaking. We are number two for takeoff. I will speak with you when we are in the air. Flight attendants, please take your seats." The attendants scurried down the aisle and locked themselves into their seats. After a brief wait, we moved. Slowly we picked up speed, and then more speed, and then lifted into the air. I looked out the window and watched the ground below me get smaller and smaller. The Boeing jet banked sharply to the left and continued to climb. I searched for the city skyline but couldn't find one. Philadelphia was buried under low clouds. I closed my window. There was nothing to see.

After a few more minutes, a *ding* was heard. The sound indicated that it was safe for passengers to move about the cabin if necessary. The flight attendants hurriedly disconnected their seat belts and made their way to the small kitchen. The flight from Philadelphia to Saint Louis was relatively short, only a couple of hours or so, and a full breakfast service and cleanup had to be accomplished, so time was of the essence. Once in Saint Louis, there was a brief layover until the plane left again, en route to Oklahoma City, its final destination.

I reclined my seat slightly and closed my eyes, my thoughts on the task that lay ahead. Without realizing it, I inhaled very deeply. I do that sometimes, almost instinctively, when pondering a big task that has to be undertaken. That's when the strong aroma of freshly brewed coffee tickled my nose. The flight attendant had arrived with her food cart.

"Good morning, what would you like to drink?" she asked.

"Coffee, please," I answered.

"Cream or sugar?" she asked.

"Both, actually," I said.

I released my tray table from its locked position and readied it for the forth-coming caffeine. She put a cup of steaming coffee on the table along with a container of cream, packets of sugar, and various sugar substitutes.

"We are serving breakfast this morning." She continued, "Would you prefer the eggs and sausage breakfast or the lighter fare?"

"The lighter fare would be fine," I answered. She bent down to the bottom of the cart and produced a tray complete with fruit, yogurt, croissant, butter, and jam.

"Thank you," I said.

"You are welcome," she replied.

She then turned to the *Wall Street Journal* man and repeated the same questions. He opted for the eggs and sausage. I nibbled on my breakfast and dozed. The flight attendant took my breakfast tray and asked if I needed anything else. I said that I was fine.

After a while, I opened my window and looked out. The sun streamed in. The sky was blue, without a cloud. I looked down to see patches of green from the abundant fields of the heartland. Finally, an announcement let us know that we had arrived in Saint Louis. We readied our seats and tray tables in preparation. After touchdown, most of the passengers got off in Saint Louis. Only a handful got on. I stayed in my seat and waited for departure. The trip to Oklahoma City was very brief, just over an hour. I was glad that I had eaten my breakfast since no meal service was provided.

I watched as the young flight attendant readied her props for the takeoff safety instructions. Already familiar with the information, I turned my attention out the window. Soon, we took off. I looked around the plane. The *Wall Street Journal* man had gotten off as had the elderly couple.

A young couple with a toddler now sat across the aisle from me. The mother searched frantically in her diaper bag for Cheerios when the baby started to cry. She found them and gave them to the little girl.

"She's teething," she apologized to me, her Oklahoma accent thick.

"She's so pretty!" I responded.

"Thank you!" the young mother beamed. The child gummed the cereal and was soon quiet.

With only forty-five minutes or so left in the flight, I shut my window shade. I closed my eyes again and let my thoughts drift. I was en route to Oklahoma City. My cherished place where I met my husband and fell in love, where I worked with people I adored, where I felt that I still belonged. I smiled as I fell asleep.

"Oh my God, oh my God!" the young mother said in alarm.

"Honey, stay calm," the man beside her said. The baby started to cry.

Abruptly awakened, I opened my eyes and looked across the aisle. I expected to see something wrong with the little girl. But, I saw immediately that everyone was looking out their windows. I opened mine and looked out, as well. Plumes of black smoke rose up from the ground.

"Sweet Jesus," I said aloud, "what is happening?"

I touched down amid total chaos. Oklahoma City had just been bombed. I watched television monitors in the airport and pieced together what had happened. I placed a call to my husband to assure him that I was OK. I then called my work. I was informed that the broadcast event had been canceled and that I should book a flight back to Pennsylvania as soon as possible. After I checked with the airline, I found that the soonest I could fly back was the following day.

With no other option available, I went to the car rental desk and got the car that had been reserved for me. I drove to the hotel that had been prearranged for me. I checked in and told the manager that I would be staying only one night instead of three. He said that he understood.

By that time, the full realization of what had occurred had been felt throughout the city and throughout the country. Every station carried the event live and updated the number of casualties and injuries with each story. A temporary morgue was set up on the scene. The number of body bags initially ordered was quickly filled. More bags were needed. It couldn't get any worse.

But, then, it did. It was discovered that the bomber was an American. He was only twenty-six years old. He was arrested later that afternoon, traveling north on Interstate 35.

I settled into my hotel room and stayed glued to the television. I felt intense sadness for the people who had died and despair for the people who had lost loved ones. But, I also felt sadness for myself. I realized that the Oklahoma City of my past was gone forever. It would never be the same: it would never be as innocent.

After a sleepless night, I traveled back to Philadelphia the next day. I hoped I could shake the depression that had taken root inside me. I was desperate to see Gino but dreaded the idea of resuming work. As I flew home, I decided that I needed to leave the job I had just taken at QVC. I didn't belong there. I didn't have any memories there.

Gino picked me up at the airport. I cried as he hugged me. We drove home and tried to speak of other things, but every conversation inevitably turned back to Oklahoma City. My depression had not lifted and it did not over the next several days. I went through the motions of life in a fog. I felt totally lost.

After several days of this behavior, Gino expressed concern. He encouraged me to turn off the television. News stations still reported live from the bombsite. A memorial service was held and it, too, was televised live. Gino suggested that we could go for a walk or go to a movie. I told him I didn't want to leave the apartment. He said he understood but suggested that I could at least go through some of the mail that had come for me. A couple of boxes and several envelopes had arrived over the past several weeks and were stacked in a corner of the living-room area. "Probably just products that vendors had sent to my home," I thought.

I couldn't think of anything I wanted to do less, but I wanted to please Gino so I turned off the television and sat down on the floor to go through the heap. Just as I thought, it was information and samples of items that I was due to sell. My depression deepened with the mere idea of going back to work. I cleaned up the mess, but then noticed a small box that still sat on the floor. It was marked "personal" and had no return address. I sat back down and opened it halfheartedly, disinterested. From the cardboard box, I pulled out a velvety pouch. I opened the pouch and pulled out a piece of jewelry. I looked at it but couldn't figure out where it had come from. There was no note to identify the sender. I put it back into the pouch and put the pouch back in the box. But then, I got it out again and looked at it more closely. That's when I started to laugh. The memory of sweatpants, no makeup, Billy Ray Cyrus-mullet hair and Joan. Joan Rivers had sent me her necklace. Maybe I did belong, after all.

It took several months for my depression to go away. I talked at length with my husband about my feelings. I even saw a psychiatrist. I was diagnosed with posttraumatic stress disorder and was treated with various medications. And, although both of those outlets were extremely helpful, I believe my recovery actually started much earlier. I believe it began with a little moment of laughter, sitting on the floor, holding a necklace.

****

What is a lifeline, really? It is different things to different people and can take many different forms. But I think I learned something very important from this experience. And it is this: Don't ever hesitate to give a kind word to someone. Don't ever hesitate to pick up the phone and call a long-lost friend or send a small gift through the mail. These simple gestures might seem insignificant to you, but, believe me, they are not. To the receiver, they might very well be a lifeline.

Big Life Lesson Number Six: Be a lifeline to a person in need and perhaps, someday, they will return the favor.

Seven:

Understanding Why You're Here.

I went to college at Oklahoma State University. Actually, I flunked out at OSU but you already know that. Anyway, the year was 1981. I lived in the girls' dormitory and was excited to start my first year of college. I had enrolled in the required classes but none of them excited me quite like my elective, Introduction to Writing. I wanted to be a writer more than anything.

I remember my professor clearly, not because he was a great teacher, but because he pretty much wore the same outfit every day. Well, that's not exactly fair. My classes with him were every Tuesday and Thursday afternoon, so maybe he just wore the same clothing twice a week, but it seemed like every day to me. His ensemble always included a crisp, starched IZOD shirt. Occasionally, the color of the shirt varied, sometimes he wore pale yellow and sometimes baby blue, but one aspect of his shirt remained consistent: the collar. It stood straight up. Like so many men of that decade, he had obviously been heavily influenced by the fashion stylings of *Miami Vice*. And the higher and stiffer the collar, the better. The points of his collar literally brushed the bottoms of his earlobes. Occasionally, he tossed a tweed jacket over the IZOD shirt. It had brown, leather elbow patches that perfectly matched his leather belt. Dark blue jeans completed his ensemble. On his feet, he wore deck shoes with no socks. Men. Go figure.

On the first day of class, I arrived with great anticipation, ready to learn all of the wisdom that he would surely impart to this would-be writer. My pencil was in hand, poised to write. I had no intention of missing anything that fell from his lips. I watched with excitement as he made his way to the blackboard. His leather elbow patches creaked slightly as he lifted his arm to write. I looked down to position my pencil onto my paper. However, no sooner had I looked down, I heard the creak of leather elbow patches again. He sat down. He was finished. He had written only four words on the blackboard. Just four. "Why are you here?" What a rip-off. What was he talking about? Was he asking why I was in that class or maybe why I had chosen that particular school? I put my pencil down. No wonder I flunked out of that college.

It's funny, though. That memory of my teacher and his question came to me recently. It all happened just a few years ago.

****

It isn't really important why I was on the train that day, just that I was there. But, I suppose a bit of background information will help make sense of this story.

I intended to get up early that morning and catch a local train from Exton, Pennsylvania, to New York City's Penn Station. It was the best way to travel to New York City from my home, given the closeness of the Exton station to where I lived. The only downside was that the local trains didn't run that often, so if you missed the one you wanted, you had to wait a long time for the next one.

That morning, I hit the snooze button twice. My husband

Gino was away on a trip and, with him gone, I fell back into my old, single-life habits. He was fastidious about promptness. Me, not so much. "Just five more minutes," I told myself, as I lay in the comfy bed. I finally got up, but then had to figure out what to wear. I tried on several outfits, but by the time I finally decided on one, I realized I had missed my local train. The next one wasn't scheduled for another two hours, far too late to get me into New York City in time for my appointment. So, with no other option available, I realized I had to drive the forty miles into Philadelphia to 30th Street Station. There, I would take a regional train into New York City. It was my least preferred way to travel into Manhattan, given the headache of fighting the traffic into Philly and the price of parking once there. Frankly, I avoided it at all costs but, that day, I had no other choice.

I was traveling to New York City to meet with a literary agent who had agreed to read some of my short stories. Although I had never spoken directly to her, we had corresponded by e-mail several times and she sounded legit. We were scheduled to meet across the street from New York's Penn Station at a specified diner around 11:00 a.m. It sounded like a good plan. So off to Philadelphia I went. I found the parking garage and punched the button that activated the automated arm that allowed me to park my car. I took my ticket and looked at it as I placed it into my handbag. Yikes, thirty-five dollars for parking. Welcome to Philadelphia.

I went into the station and found my train. I boarded and took the travel time to arrange my short stories. I wanted to be organized when I met the agent. An hour or so later, I arrived in New York. Through a maze of people and various corridors, I finally found the exit. I pushed through double doors, exited the station, and made my way across the street. I was just in time for my appointment.

I entered the diner and looked around for the agent. As you already know, I had never met her face to face, but I assumed that she would be a professional-looking lady. I looked for someone who matched that description, but found no one. I checked my watch. It was about 10:55. I noticed a sign that indicated that customers should seat themselves. "I might as well get a table," I thought. I found one close to the entrance and sat down. As I looked down to rummage through my handbag for my cell phone, I felt a presence approach the table. "Oh, great," I thought, "she is here." I looked up and anticipated the official introduction of the agent but, instead, found myself looking directly at a grumpy waitress.

"What'll you have?" she mumbled. She was an older woman. Her gray hair was piled high on top of her head and was held into place by a tight, black hairnet. She wore a red and white checkered blouse and a black skirt. Over her skirt was a waitress apron, slightly soiled.

"Oh, I haven't seen a menu yet," I responded. She sighed heavily, reached across the table and produced a menu. The tattered, plastic-coated, tri-fold menu had been wedged between the ketchup and the maple syrup. I had not noticed it there. She plopped it down in front of me.

I opened the menu and scanned the breakfast specials. Omelets, pancakes, waffles, cream-chipped beef over toast. Standard diner fare. In all honesty, I wasn't hungry or thirsty but I did need to buy some time as I waited for the agent to arrive. The waitress stood over me and pressed me for an order. I asked for coffee, four dollars, and a fruit cup, eight dollars and fifty cents, the two cheapest items on the menu.

"Is that it?" she frowned. She didn't bother to write down my order on the little notepad she had just taken from her apron. I nodded. A few minutes later, she delivered my meager meal. As she was about to turn and leave, I asked for cream for my coffee. From her apron she produced two individual creamers, slightly warm. I opened them and poured them in. Then, I looked down to inspect my fruit cup. Well, they certainly hadn't exaggerated the name of the dish. A coffee cup filled with large cubes of apples and a few slices of banana sat in front of me. Two, maybe three bites at the most, I estimated.

"You pay up front," she said as she left my bill facedown on the table. She walked away. I looked at the bill. With tax and tip, I was out about sixteen dollars for lukewarm coffee and several-days-old fruit. Welcome to New York.

I ate as slowly as humanly possible. I looked around for the literary agent who still had not arrived. I called her cell phone several times but only got her voice mail. She had not attempted to call me either, by the silence of my cell phone. After forty-five minutes of waiting, I gave up. The agent was obviously not coming. Add to that, the lunch crowd had arrived and the hair-net-wearing, grumpy waitress eyed my table. I didn't need anyone to spell it out for me. I had been stood up. I paid my bill and walked back across the street to Penn Station. There, I bought a return ticket for Philadelphia. I planned to retrieve my car as quickly as possible and drive straight home.

There weren't many travelers that day, which was fine with me. After I cooled my heels in the main waiting area for a while, my train was called. I found my gate, went down the escalator, and located my train. The conductor stood just outside the first car.

"All aboard, all aboard!" he shouted. He was a big man, more than six feet tall and almost as broad. He stood with a wide stance, as if ready to spring into action if needed. His navy-blue jacket strained against his midsection. Two gold-tone buttons looked like they were about to pop off.

I boarded the train with the other passengers and walked through the cars until I found a desirable seat. You see, first-time travelers often take the first seats they see. Seasoned travelers, however, know to continue walking through the cars to find more solitude. That's what I did. I walked down to the next-to-last car and saw that it was empty. I sat down. The public address system squawked to life. Announcements reminded passengers of the train that they were on and the stops that would be made. We were asked to have our tickets out for collection.

The train slowly lumbered its way toward the tunnel. I closed my eyes. After a moment or two, I heard a bit of noise coming from the other end of the car. "Probably another passenger," I thought to myself. It was not uncommon for passengers to change seats even after travel had started, sometimes to stretch out or perhaps seek a bit more privacy. I did it often myself when a car was a bit too crowded for my liking.

Suddenly, I felt a tap on my shoulder. I looked up.

"Ticket, please." The conductor loomed overhead.

"Oh, so sorry," I said. I handed him my ticket. *Click, click, click.* He hole-punched it, tore off his part, and put it in his pocket. The other part of the ticket he placed above my seat.

"Have a nice day, Miss," he said in a tired voice. He walked slowly down the aisle and took off his conductor's hat as he walked. He massaged his forehead vigorously before he put his hat back on. I wondered how many trips he had already taken that day. He continued all the way down the aisle without stopping until he reached the other end of the car. I watched as he stopped at the very end of the car. "Yes," I thought, "I was right; another passenger had entered the car while my eyes were closed." From my vantage point, I could not see the other passenger's face, only the back of the head. But I assumed it was a woman due to the blonde, curly hair that I saw. The conductor took her ticket, punched it, tore off his part, and then put her part above her seat, just as he had done mine. He then exited. I anticipated a quiet trip, with only two of us in the car.

The train picked up speed as it traveled deep into the tunnel. The car was dim, except for the reading lights that had been left on by previous passengers. All around me, spotlights shined down onto empty seats. I looked out the window but saw nothing. Then suddenly, the car was flooded with sunlight. We had just crossed under the river and were now in New Jersey. I settled back and looked out at the passing scenery. There were only two stops before mine. Newark, and then Trenton. After Philadelphia, the train continued on to Wilmington, Baltimore, and, finally, Washington, DC. I looked out of the window and sighed. What a wasted day.

I would love to have called Gino, but, as you know, he was out of town. He was on a much-deserved vacation. He had traveled to Oklahoma several days earlier to spend time with family and friends. He was due back the next morning. I could certainly wait till then to tell him the events of the day. To pass the time, I decided to read a book. I located it in my handbag and found my place.

I had only read through a couple of pages when I heard the most peculiar sound. Kind of like the hiss of an angry cat combined with the screech of an owl. So much for a quiet ride. It was obvious that the other rider in the car had brought an animal onboard. After several more minutes of the sound, I could wait no longer. I had to see what it was. I decided I would pretend that I had to go to the ladies' room. I got my bag and got up out of my seat. I walked slowly. I did not want to miss the opportunity to see what was creating the horrific noise. As I moved closer to the sound, I glanced to the left and saw the back of the head of the lady. She looked at something to the right, something that was in the large open space reserved for wheelchairs. I followed the direction of her gaze and also looked to the right. What I saw took my breath away. It wasn't an animal that made the noise. It was a little girl.

I don't know exactly what was wrong with her. I only know that I had never seen such deformities. I placed her at around six years of age. She sat in a sort of stroller, just like the ones that infants use, but much bigger to accommodate her size. The stroller had a headrest that leaned far back. That would explain why I had not seen her until that moment. Her head was at least double the size it should have been. Her eyes sat on the far side of her head. Her ears were misshapen mounds of flesh. Her mouth was open. From it came the sounds that had drawn me from my seat. The blonde curls that capped her head seemed like a cruel joke. I hesitated for only a moment. I walked the few additional steps to the bathroom and went in. I made sure the door was shut before I sat down on the closed toilet seat. The train swayed. I felt ill.

I stayed in the ladies' room as long as I could and prepared to return to my seat when my cell phone rang. It was Gino. He had decided to come home earlier than planned. In fact, he was coming home that very evening. He asked if I would pick him up at the American Airlines terminal in Philadelphia. I assured him that I would be there. Although I was only half listening, I got all the necessary information from Gino, wished him a good flight, and said good-bye. I left the ladies' room and returned to my seat. The little girl had stopped crying. She was silent for the rest of the trip.

After stops in Newark and Trenton, we arrived into

Philadelphia's 30th Street Station. I collected my things and walked to the exit just behind me. I didn't want to walk past the little girl again. My intention was to go straight to the parking garage, get my car, and then drive to the airport to wait for Gino's flight. The train came to a complete stop and the doors slid open. I stepped off the train, onto the platform, and looked for the escalator. 30th Street Station is constructed like most big city train stations. The trains actually enter the station underground. Passengers are then required to take stairs or an escalator to the main terminal.

I finally found the sign indicating the up-escalator. I walked toward it and noticed that the lady and the little girl had exited the train, as well. They waited as the conductor took their bags off the train. He placed the luggage on the floor of the platform. Although her back was to me, I could tell that the lady was trying to speak to the conductor. He faced me and I could tell that he was clearly confused. He shook his head as she continued to talk, his brow furrowed. As I got closer, I understood why. She spoke a foreign language. I guessed it to be Russian. The conductor edged slowly away from her. She spoke even louder. She was openly distraught. She looked around in a panic and gestured to him. She did not understand why he was getting back on the train, leaving her there. She did not know that the train was about to leave again to continue its route toward Washington. In fact, passengers from Philadelphia had begun to board the train. The platform filled, the noise level increased. The conductor looked at his watch. He edged further away from her and soon passengers filled the space between them. The lady continued to yell loudly. She raised herself up as high as she could on her tiptoes and tried to see where the conductor had gone.

People pushed to get to the train before it left. The lady

finally realized that the conductor was not coming back. She desperately tried to reposition the child's wheelchair, which had been sitting in the middle of the platform along with their luggage. She pushed and pulled the chair until the little girl was pointed toward a cement wall. She turned away from the child to get the bags when someone accidentally bumped the child's wheelchair. The little girl wailed. It was the same sound I had heard on the train. I could no longer stand it. I approached the lady and tapped her on the shoulder.

"Excuse me," I said.

She turned and looked at me. For the first time, I really saw her face. She was much older than I originally thought. She had blonde, slightly curly hair, very fair skin, and brown eyes. And a look of exhaustion that I had never seen on another human being.

"Can I help you?" I asked. She looked at me quizzically.

"I'll get a redcap," I said. She didn't understand.

"I will help you," I said. "Follow me." Although I knew she didn't fully understand my words, she seemed to sense that I offered assistance. She nodded and got behind the little girl's stroller. She pushed the child with one hand and picked up a bag with the other. I picked up her other two bags and carried them along with my own handbag. We walked to the far end of the platform where the elevator was located. After pushing the button, we waited for the elevator doors to open. We entered and waited for the elevator doors to close. The lady was silent. I snuck a glance at her. She looked at the child with an expression that can only be described as sadness combined with resentment. Finally, we were at the main floor. My plan was to go to customer service and see if I could find someone who could act as a translator. We exited the elevator and stopped for a moment. The lady motioned to me that she needed to get into one of the bags that I carried, so I handed it to her. She looked inside and got out several pieces of paper with foreign writing on them. As she read through the papers, I changed places with her, got behind the wheelchair, and pushed the child. Unfortunately, we had to walk across the entire expanse of the main floor to get to customer service. The whispers and stares were heartbreaking. I saw expressions of sheer horror as passengers and employees looked at the little girl. Slowly, their gaze traveled up to my face as if to say, "Oh, you poor, poor woman." They thought I was her mother. I wanted to scream, "She's not mine! I am not her mother." I immediately felt a rush of shame. My eyes watered. I pitied the child and loathed myself.

After what felt like an eternity, we finally got to the customer-service counter. An employee approached and asked if she could help. I briefly explained the situation and asked if there was anyone on staff who could act as a translator.

"What language?" the agent asked.

"I don't know for sure," I said, "but my guess is Russian." She picked up the house phone and asked to be connected to someone. She asked that he come to customer service. After some time, a male agent, presumably the person she had called, appeared. Tentatively at first, he spoke to the lady. She instantly responded. She gestured to the girl and spoke even faster. He nodded and listened. She showed him the papers that she had just gotten out of the bag. He read them over and handed them back to her. He spoke, pointed to the papers that he had just returned to her, and then pointed to a clock on the wall. He shook his head. Her face fell. She spoke again, her words came in a rush, her desperation was palpable.

"What is it?" I asked the man. "What's wrong?" He looked at me.

"Your friend is trying to get the little girl to a medical specialist and she just missed her connection," he said. "I was just explaining to her that she would have to wait until the next train."

"Which train did she miss?" I asked.

"The shuttle," he said.

"The shuttle to where?" I pressed him.

"To the airport," he said. Just where I was going.

I took the lady and the little girl to the airport. I carried their bags into the terminal and checked them in. I pointed them toward the security checkpoint as I explained their situation to airport personnel. I was assured that they would make their flight to Boston.

If this story had a Hollywood ending, the lady, at the very last minute, would have turned back to me as she made her way toward her gate. Her eyes would have been filled with grateful tears and she would have blown me a big kiss. But that is not how it ended. I watched as she walked down the concourse toward her gate. She pushed the stroller with one hand and carried her handbag with the other. Her focus was solely on protecting the child. She never looked back.

****

If you are a spiritual person, you probably read the Bible. I do. And, there is one verse that I think often. It talks about all things working together for good. And, I guess that's right. You see, I never heard from that literary agent. I never found out why she stood me up that day. It's as if she disappeared right off the face of the planet. But it doesn't really matter. What matters is that I was in the right place at exactly the right time.

It all makes me think about that question my professor

posed to me more than twenty-five years ago. Why am I here? To be a writer? Perhaps. Or maybe not. Maybe I am just here to be a servant. To carry bags, push strollers, and be a taxi driver. To do whatever is needed to make it better for someone else.

So, IZOD-wearing, collar-up teacher, wherever you are, I have finally answered your question.

Big Life Lesson Number Seven: Don't worry so much about understanding why you're here. When the time is right, God will let you know.

EIGHT:

Seeing Clearly.

Having just moved to Manhattan, Gino and I quickly learned that it's all about transportation. How to get from point A to point B as quickly as possible. And, as you might expect, in a place as diverse as New York City, there are numerous options. Here are a few.

The car service. The crème de la crème of transport. Nothing quite compares to a black Lincoln Town Car, complete with hatted driver, taking you to your desired destination. Exceptionally luxurious and very expensive, this is an option I never use, unless, of course, someone else is paying.

The taxi. Simply stated, the luck of the draw. Sometimes you're fortunate and you get a newer vehicle with a pine fragrance wafting through the air. But more often than not, you get the taxi that somehow missed the mandatory "someone just puked in the backseat" cleaning. It is the same vehicle that, try as you might, you can't get the back windows to roll down.

The subway. Two words. Urine stench.

The bus. Prompt, mostly clean, and climate controlled, it was my favorite option until recently when an unaccompanied fourteen-year-old, who sat behind me, repeatedly punched the Stop Requested button. The driver stopped at every corner despite the fact that no one got off. This went on for seventeen blocks.

The pedicab. That contraption that combines a rickshaw with a bicycle. I haven't tried this one and I don't think I will. I'm sorry, I just can't imagine sitting there as the pedaler, whose butt is conveniently pointed directly at me, strains to get up a steep hill.

So, you can see why walking is my favorite way of getting around. In fact, unless you are physically unable, walking is the one guaranteed way of getting to your desired destination on time. And, if you are frugal like me, it also has another appeal. It's free. I love to walk and I do it every day. It clears my head and increases my heart rate. So, with all this walking, it was just a matter of time before I began to notice something rather odd. I call it the crosswalk phenomenon.

It starts simply enough. A small crowd of people gather on a corner, waiting for the crosswalk to give them permission to cross the street. A few seconds pass and, invariably, someone in the group steps out onto the street, looking for a break in the traffic so that he can quickly dart across. Others at the corner, seeing the first guy, attempt the same thing, doing anything they can to get across the street ahead of everyone else. They are the impatient ones.

Meanwhile, others have joined the crowd. This group stands slightly away from the curb to avoid any soiling of their perfectly tailored suits. They do not attempt to conceal their expression of disdain. Obviously, their car service has run late and they have been forced to walk. They answer their cell phones or check their text messages. They are unwilling to move until they are good and ready. They are the arrogant ones.

And, still another group has joined the ever-growing crowd at the corner, especially in New York City. This group consists of people who carry cameras around their necks and are so busy looking up at the city sights that they are oblivious to everything around them. Anything that twinkles takes their attention away. They are the easily distracted ones.

And here's the irony. As the impatient ones look right and left to see if they can scramble across, as the arrogant ones look down to check their oh-so-important text messages, and as the easily distracted ones look up to take yet another picture, the crosswalk has changed.

If they had all simply been looking in the right direction, they could have all been walking.

Sometimes we are so eager looking for answers in other directions that we miss what is clearly in front of us. It reminds me of something that happened some time ago. A simple little story that taught me a very important life lesson. And it all began with a promise I made to my parents.

****

It is very rare that Mama and Daddy ask me for anything, so a couple of years ago when they called and asked for a favor, I was all too happy to oblige. It was a simple enough request: would I be the keynote speaker at a ladies' event at my daddy's church? I said that I would be happy to do so.

"But, what should I talk about?" I asked my daddy during the phone call.

"Well, how about 'The Meaning of True Success'?" he suggested. While Daddy wanted me to think that he selected this subject matter because he had complete confidence in me, I secretly wondered if it was because the number of letters in the title would fit neatly on the kiosk in front of his church in Summerville, Georgia. A pretty little town, Summerville is located in the northern part of Georgia, about a day-and-a-half's drive from my home in New York. He waited for my answer. Unfortunately, for me, I always crack under the pressure of phone silence. I agreed to the subject matter. Just then, Mama got on the line. She was thrilled that I had agreed. She went on to say that the admission charge would be a modest three dollars. Wow! I was less valuable than a caramel macchiato from Starbucks.

"Now, Lisa, you know that you are worth a lot more than that," she seemed to read my thoughts. "It's just that this is a ministry and we want to collect only enough money to cover the costs of the ...."

"Chips, dips, and finger sandwiches?" I finished her sentence. In the event that you did not grow up in the South, here is a little-known fact. Almost every Sunday night, the church program ended with chips, dips, and finger sandwiches. In fact, when I was a little girl I thought it was all one word. Chipsdipsandfingersandwiches. And, mind you, not just any chips, dips, or finger sandwiches, but ones that were very sweet or, at least, contained enough fat to satisfy the food pyramid's fat zone for the entire week. The array was vast as one enjoyed an endless table filled with sandwiches of sweet, honey-roasted pork or syrupy, barbecue chicken. Occasionally, you found lean, white meat turkey but only if it was smothered with creamy, full-fat American cheese.

The chips were also specially selected. My particular favorites were corn chips and cheese doodles but barbecue chips, Pringles, and the ever-popular CornNuts were also available. Triscuits and other fatty crackers were thrown in for good measure, as well.

The big deal, however, was the dip. Bean, Ranch, French, yes, those were occasionally seen, but any good Southern person knew that it was perfectly acceptable to whip up a thick, meaty chili and call it a dip. You could always expect to see several blocks of Velveeta tossed into a crock pot. They simmered, golden yellow, and invited chips to be plunged in. One of the best dips I ever had wasn't a dip at all but rather a cheese ball covered with Georgia pecans, but because it could be smeared on a cracker, it qualified as a dip.

Not all dips were well received, however. I recall one church event when one of the attendees brought a picante sauce. Not only was it *not* sweet, it didn't have a smidgen of fat in it. It was evident that people had sampled it throughout the evening. There were traces of chips and remnants of other dips that floated in the tomato mixture, but it was obviously not to the liking of the church members. At the end of the evening, it was the only dip left. I dumped out what remained of the sad, little, fat-free picante, washed the bowl, and waited for the owner to retrieve it. They never came back. I hope that they found another church so that their soul wasn't in jeopardy due to a dip.

So, there I was, with a speaking engagement assigned to me by my parents. I needed to collect my thoughts and prepare a speech, but every time I tried to identify what defined a successful life, I got stuck. My definition of success sounded more like a laundry list of outward accomplishments. It sounded empty and self-serving. I was getting nowhere fast. So, I did what any smart person would do. I asked other people. I queried close friends and casual acquaintances alike and they all came up with the same answer: they didn't quite know either. Sure, suggestions were made. One friend said it had to do with accomplishing your professional goals. Kind of what I had already come up with. Another said it had to do with being influential within your community. That one sounded a bit like politics (yawn). Finally, I knew I was on the wrong track when one acquaintance, from New York City, said success was when you knew which shoes to wear with which outfit. She went on to say that it was important that I throw around names like Badgley Mischka and Christian Lacroix during my speech. Well, I couldn't see that definition going over very well with the ladies of Summerville, Georgia, esteemed Daughters of the Confederate. I could literally imagine the rustling and whispering as the ladies would turn to each other and asked, "What IS she talking about?"

It seemed that there was an epidemic of people who didn't have a clue as to what success was all about. And, time was running out. It had been several months since that initial phone call from my parents and I was no further along on my speech. Although I still had no presentation, Gino and I made our plans to leave for Summerville. And, since we were driving, we decided to leave a few days early and stop off at our little apartment in Ocean City, Maryland. You see, we had vacationed in Ocean City frequently over the years. So often, in fact, that we decided to buy a one-bedroom apartment there so that we could come and go as often as we wanted. We had owned the apartment for quite a while and had spent lots of time there, but we were still in the process of going through the things that the previous owners had left behind. As in most real estate transactions of its kind, we had purchased the apartment completely furnished, outfitted with everything. Now came the task of discarding what we didn't need and adding what we did need.

So, we went to our little place. I had high hopes that the roaring waves, white sand, and blue skies would give me inspiration. No such luck. I considered calling my daddy to tell him I just couldn't do it. But then, he would have to remove the words "Join host Lisa Mason as she discusses 'Defining True Success'!" from his beloved kiosk and replace them with the words "Event Canceled." He would never be able to hold his head up in Summerville again, not to mention the hassle my mama would have trying to organize another event for the use of all those chips, dips, and finger sandwiches.

On the last day of our vacation there, Gino left the apartment ahead of me to get the car. He asked me to hurry along since we were already behind schedule. I was in the process of rolling my small suitcase down a long hallway to the front door when the sound of breaking glass startled me. It had come from behind me. I looked around. A picture, hanging on the wall, had fallen to the floor. In my haste, I must have brushed it with my shoulder. That would explain the sound I heard. I was just about to walk to the kitchen to fetch a broom and dustpan when something stopped me.

"That's odd," I muttered to myself. I looked at the place where the picture had been hanging. The color behind it was completely different from the color of the rest of the wall. It seemed that past owners had never taken it down when they selected a new paint color. They just painted around it.

I got the broom and dustpan and bent over to sweep the whole mess up. In all honesty, I wasn't upset about it. It was a picture that I had intended to throw away anyway. The frame was splintered and cracked in several places and the picture was nothing special. It was a generic beach scene and had several handwritten lines of text across the bottom. The handwriting was small and unattractive, with letters squeezed so tightly next to each other that I had decided that it was not worth my time or effort to decipher. I picked the pieces of frame up off the floor and tossed them into the trash. I began brushing the shards of broken glass into the dustpan, and was about to throw the silly picture away as well, when something caught my eye.

The word: Success. That word, along with other words, had been handwritten on the bottom of the picture. I brought it closer and read:

Success.

To laugh often and much.

To win the respect of intelligent people and the affection of children.

To earn the appreciation of honest critics and endure the betrayal of false friends.

To appreciate beauty.

To find the best in others.

To leave the world a bit better, whether by a healthy child, a garden path or a redeemed social condition.

To know that even one life has breathed easier because you have lived.

This is to have succeeded.

—Ralph Waldo Emerson

"Well, hello Mr. Emerson," I said to myself. "You have just saved my life." It was the perfect text for my ladies' talk. I prepared an hour-long presentation using Emerson's points and received a standing ovation at the conclusion of the event. Best of all, according to my mother, the attendees raved over the assortment of dips, chips, and finger sandwiches that followed.

****

I told this story to a friend recently. She said how lucky I was to have found the text in the nick of time. But the truth is, the poem had been there all along. It had been hanging on that wall, in that exact same spot, the whole time that Gino and I had occupied the apartment. It had, in fact, held that place of distinction for years. Past owners must have treasured it so much that they never took it from its rightful place. Yet I walked right past it numerous times, never aware that it existed. Never knowing that the very text I was looking for was right under my nose.

I guess I was kind of like those people at the crosswalk. Too impatient, arrogant, or easily distracted to see what was right in front of me.

Big Life Lesson Number Eight: Sometimes, what you so desperately seek, you already have.

NINE:

Looking Beyond The Obvious.

I learned of the film only recently. At first, I didn't quite believe it. I assumed that someone had exaggerated its existence or that I had misunderstood what was told to me.

But at a recent family reunion, my Aunt Verleen brought a magazine for me to see. In it, an article confirmed the release of the movie. You can look it up on the Internet, if you wish: IronCityBlues.com. But, in the event that you don't want to search for it, I will hit the high points for you.

It seems that a musician by the name of Big Mike Griffin heard about Iron City, Tennessee, and its reputation. Wanting to see the town for himself, Big Mike, along with a camera crew, traveled to Iron City. There, he interviewed townspeople and documented the decay that has become a part of the landscape. After a short time, he packed up his belongings and left town. Later, he released his film. In it, Iron City is called untamed and lawless; its residents, a group of people who live on the edge of anarchy.

I am not debating the content of the film. The truth is Big Mike has the right to say anything he wants to say about Iron City. He took an interest in a little community and decided to write about it. In a way, I commend him. I have always admired people who take the time to learn about tiny, out-of-the-way places and then share their experiences with others. But, I do have one big problem with his film. Mike never lived in Iron City. He has absolutely no history with the place. But I do.

****

Iron City, Tennessee, population 350 or so, sits just over the Alabama line and is just about 100 miles south of Nashville. From Nashville, Highway 31 takes you to State Road 43, which takes you as far as Saint Joseph, Tennessee. At that point, however, familiarity is required to recall exactly which road takes you the rest of the way into Iron City.

It's a single-lane road that twists through hills and valleys. The road is dotted with potholes that have been patched and patched again. Dense trees and brush make it hard to determine if the few structures that still stand are inhabited or vacant. Homemade footbridges are positioned over numerous streams that flow down the mountain. Those bridges are covered with moss. They are rarely used these days. They are connected to paths that seem to trail off to nowhere.

And then, after several more miles and up one last turn, Iron City is revealed. A tiny town, it is nestled among trees. It sits between sharp and unyielding bluffs. A lone gas station greets visitors, with a single neon sign that proclaims that Sun Drop, the local soft drink of choice, is served there. As you drive further, the main street is revealed. The storefront windows are boarded up or broken out. The school has long since closed down, due to a lack of students. Numerous houses sit vacant and give the impression that the inhabitants left in a hurry. There is no money to repair and no motivation to demolish, so structures have fallen prey first to vandalism, then to animals and, finally, time. Like so many small towns across America, Iron City has changed drastically in the past decades. Industry has come and gone. Residents have become discouraged and left the area completely. Unemployment rates have swelled to nearly fourteen percent at times. To an outsider, it resembles a ghost town. But, remember, I am not an outsider.

It was the birthplace of my parents, Paul and Barbara Mason, and the starting point of my life as well. At one time, it was a thriving little community, filled with civic pride, overflowing with workers. It was a place that people loved to visit because of the beauty of the streams and the lushness of the vegetation. There was a time when schoolchildren walked to and from school and laughed with each other. The churches burst at the seams as summer revivals were held, and baptisms were conducted either in the church baptisteries or at one of the numerous bodies of clean, clear water nearby.

My daddy, Paul Henry Mason, was raised in Iron City primarily by his mother, Eula. Although it is now gone, he lived in a single-story wooden house that sat on the outskirts of town. The house was overshadowed by a steep hill that loomed just behind it, keeping it cool, even in the heat of summer. In the winter, the house was heated by a single pot-bellied stove. The wooden floors were cracked and uneven, due to age and a flood, years earlier. A dirt road ran in front of the house. On the other side of the dirt road were the railroad tracks that ran parallel. For many years, railroad cars traveled up and down those tracks and moved materials between major cities. Just down the dirt road from my daddy's house sat a row of one-room shanties. They had been hastily constructed for the people who had come to work in Iron City after iron ore was discovered there, thus the name.

My daddy was one of four children. All four children were under the age of seven when my grandfather abruptly left the family. So, Grandmother Mason went to work at the Iron City café to feed the children. She waitressed or was the short-order cook, whatever was needed. In her absence, the children played carefully, since each only had one pair of pants to last through the school year. If any of them tore their britches, they would have to wear them that way for the whole year. Sometimes they sustained themselves solely on biscuits and gravy and whatever Grandmother could bring home from the restaurant. In her rare, spare moments, Grandmother Mason tended her flowers that flowed from pots on her front porch. Her porch swing was always filled with some neighbor or another who stopped over to say hello or just discuss the weather. They all attended the First Baptist Church every Sunday, no exceptions.

Just a stone's throw away, in the center of town, my mama was raised. Barbara June Mashburn was also one of four children. She grew up in a two-story, white house and was also raised primarily by her mother, Pearl. Grandmother Mashburn also went to work to support the family. At that time, the main street was the location of several businesses. One of them was a grocery and sundry store. Grandmother Mashburn was a cashier and always greeted the customers with courtesy and patience. My grandmother loved to travel the several miles to a location where she had discovered natural spring water that bubbled up from the ground. She and my mama took containers and filled them to the very top, careful not to spill any. Once home, the spring water was used for drinking and hair washing.

Grandmother allowed Mama to visit the bookmobile. Mama waited on pins and needles as the van arrived each week. It carried a new supply of books, and since there was no library in Iron City, it was the next best thing. The books were delivered to the Iron City barbershop, so Mama tiptoed in, amidst men and pipe smoke, and quickly grabbed any book she could. She and the other children attended the Free Will Baptist Church every Sunday. No exceptions.

Eventually, Paul and Barbara met. They married and had every intention of staying in Iron City, content in the routine that had been instilled in them over the years. In fact, for a short while, they lived in the Iron City boarding house, a small structure that primarily provided housing to the railroad workers. Within several months of their marriage, Mama found out that she was expecting. My sister Missy was born and, about two years later, me. We were surrounded by family and found ourselves spending time with our beloved grandmothers.

I remember rocking back and forth on Grandmother Mason's front porch swing, lazily watching the bees buzzing around her flowers, as she told me tales of her youth. She would stop her stories occasionally and give a hearty wave when a worker or a town person would walk past her house. We watched the trains go past and tried to guess where they might be going.

Inside her house, she kept an extensive collection of dolls. Occasionally, she let Missy and me play with them, but only if we were very careful, since they were precious porcelain. She had a true feather bed. Not one made by a factory, but one made the old-fashioned way. We slept on it when we stayed over at her house.

My memories of Grandmother Mashburn are just as strong. I recall meals at her house very clearly. She used whatever she could find in the pantry to put food on each plate. From scratch she prepared the most incredible butter beans. Soft, meaty, and flavorful, they simmered all day long and created a thick, luscious sauce. Her corn bread was light and sweet and needed nothing added to it. She cut generous squares and placed them on a platter. To her, it was probably meager and pitiful; to me, it was bountiful and delicious.

Lisa Mason

Occasionally I was allowed to go down to the store while she worked. Despite her protests, I took my shoes off immediately when I entered the store. The old wood floor was cool and had been walked on for so many years that it felt like polished stone beneath my feet.

When I was allowed to stay at her house, I looked forward to her nightly beauty ritual. She would come into the front room in her housecoat and tell Missy and me Bible stories. All the while, she massaged Pond's cold cream onto her face. Later, she tissued it off and sent us to bed. But the heavenly fragrance of the cold cream lingered in the house for hours and, sometimes, I was able to smell it on my clothes the following day.

Mama and Daddy's siblings also got married and had children. We all lived in very close proximity to each other, so meals were often eaten together and holidays were celebrated. My sister and I often spent the night at my Aunt Patsy's house when Mama and Daddy were away. She let us sleep in the guest bedroom, which was my favorite room in which to sleep because the headboard had two lights built right in. My sister and I had the most fun as we turned the lights on and off. We pretended that they were spotlights for our Broadway show. I suspect many a night Aunt Patsy had to come into our room to turn off the headboard lights after we had fallen asleep. My Uncle Carl, Patsy's husband, worked the third shift at the local factory. Just about the time Missy and I woke up, Uncle Carl got home. So, we all sat down to breakfast and ate eggs, bacon, sausage, biscuits, and gravy as Uncle Carl launched into some wonderful tall tale. To this day, I believe that he is one of the best storytellers I have ever known.

It's true. All of this happened a long, long time ago. The Iron City of my youth is officially gone. All that is left of it is a collection of memories. But, doesn't that count a little bit? Aren't there times when the present should be balanced with a tiny bit of the past to paint a more accurate picture? I believe so.

This reminds me of my friend, Fran. I met her shortly after Gino and I moved to New York City. Although she lived on my same street, the only thing we had in common was a zip code, and barely that. I lived in a high-rise building with a marble lobby and multiple elevators. A doorman greeted me every time I entered the building, eager to open the door and welcome me home. Noise was kept strictly at a minimum in my building so that residents could live in a peaceful environment.

She lived at the end of my block in a single room just above a Japanese restaurant, no elevator, no doorman. She walked up five flights to her studio. She never invited me to her apartment. She said that even though she lived on the top floor, the air still smelled heavily of fish from the restaurant below. She had no money to run her air conditioner, so with the windows ajar, her room was filled with the sounds of late-night revelers and honking horns, she told me.

The main entrance to the Japanese restaurant faced a major street in Manhattan. A trendy, hip eatery, the awning proclaimed its name in bold colors. Outside tables and chairs gave an appearance of chic elegance as white-shirted, bow-tied waiters scurried around to please patrons. The menu was expensive. It consisted of various types of sushi and assorted Japanese dishes. Beautifully dressed guests bustled in and out at all hours. Occasionally, paparazzi snapped a picture of one celebrity or another who dined there.

The employee entrance to the restaurant was around the corner, on a side street, the same street as where I lived. That employee entrance was also the same doorway that provided access to Fran's hallway and staircase. She sat on the stoop of that employees' entrance the day I met her.

"Have a light, lovey?" she asked. I was racing to get to the subway stop that morning and was deep in my own thoughts. I was startled by the sound of her voice. I slowed my pace slightly and glanced over at her. I guessed her to be in her late seventies, but it was hard to be sure. Her green eyes twinkled as she looked at me. She had a cigarette poised in her fingers. She smiled. She was missing most of her teeth.

"Oh," I said, "I'm sorry. I don't smoke."

"Not a problem, Dearie," she said. She sounded as if she were from England or perhaps Scotland. I waved and walked on. Thus became our ritual for several weeks. She would ask for a light each day I walked past her, and each time, I would remind her that I didn't smoke.

Over time, I stopped and talked with her a bit more. I asked how she was and how her day was going. It was all very surface and, frankly, very pleasant. She was one of the most cheerful people I had ever met. I began to notice that I was just one of many people who stopped to talk. She seemed to know everyone by their name and they, hers.

It was during one of my brief conversations with her that the Japanese restaurant owner approached her and asked her to move off of the stoop. He said she was in the way of his employees. She looked around at the totally empty area and smiled as if to say, "What employees?" It was clear that the restaurant owner was embarrassed that she sat there. He was afraid that his chic patrons would be offended by her appearance. So, she got up. She went into the entrance and up her staircase. I watched her go.

That night I had a very vivid dream. I dreamed that I took a newspaper and stuffed it down the restaurant owner's throat. He struggled repeatedly, but still I would not let up. I was determined that he would never speak again. When I awoke the next morning, I felt shame and confusion about my dream. But it proved to be prophetic, in a way. It was in a newspaper that I read of her death some months later.

She was from Ireland. She had been an actress and had died of cancer. The obituary summed her existence up in a few sentences, but I suspect that her life had been much more full, much more wonderful than I would ever know. I suspect that she had been an incredibly strong woman who had gone through the final months of her life alone, knowing the end was near, and still she took the time to smile and make idle chitchat with people, like me, on the street. I also suspect that one of the greatest joys in her final days was to simply sit on that stoop and watch children and puppies and parents alike as they went through their day. I wanted to make thousands of copies of her obituary and paste them onto the windows of the Japanese restaurant so that the pretentious, snotty patrons would know just how wonderful she had been. But, of course, I didn't.

The truth is, this story isn't really about Big Mike making a film about Iron City. And I guess it really isn't about my friend Fran, either. I guess it is about judgment and how dangerous and unfair it can be.

****

We all pass judgment, every day. Sometimes we do it consciously, sometimes not, but we do it. With little more than a brief glance, we size up a place or a person and, in one fell swoop, we determine their worth and their subsequent importance in this world. But every broken-down person, every deserted little town has a back story. A history that deserves to be honored and remembered.

When you take the time to look beyond the obvious, you see the glory days of the past. You also see the potential of the future.

Big Life Lesson Number Nine: Take the time to look beyond the obvious. Because someday, someone might have to 'look beyond the obvious' when looking at you.

TEN:

Moving On.

Ⓘt's a concept that has been ingrained in each of us from a very early age. Getting permission to leave. You remember: raising your hand during grade school to go to the restroom. Waiting until the nurse brings the dismissal slip from the doctor. We have all been conditioned to wait until someone in authority gives us the approval to move on. Sometimes, as in the examples above, it is necessary. But sometimes, it is detrimental.

I found myself thinking about this subject recently. Not because of something that had happened to me, but because of something I overheard.

****

I pried the lid off of my coffee cup that afternoon in anticipation of the cream and sugar I was about to stir in. The small counter, where the condiments were located, was crowded, at least three deep. People pushed in to doctor up their beverages. I waited. I wasn't in a hurry. In fact, I knew that I would be hanging out for at least the next twenty-five minutes, so I allowed others to reach around me for their napkins, stirrers, Splenda, etc.

Finally, the crowd lessened. I stepped up and sat my cup

down on the counter. I reached for the stainless-steel thermos that proclaimed "half and half" on the outside. I shook it. Empty.

I looked around. As if reading my mind, a Starbucks employee walked toward me with another thermos.

"Thank you," I said as she sat the new thermos down and tidied up the counter. She nodded but said nothing. I poured in my cream and added sugar. I stirred and sipped. Perfect. That task accomplished, I set my mind on my next assignment. I needed to find a table. I scanned the eatery and looked for a spot. Nothing open, but I noticed two girls in the far corner seemed to be getting ready to leave. I edged closer to their table.

This particular Starbucks was one that I frequented often. Located at Penn Station in New York City, it is on the lower level close to the A, C, and E subway lines. It was also very close to the Long Island Railroad and Amtrak, so it proved a central location when I waited for someone who was traveling on one of those trains. The only downside was the crowds. In addition to folks like me, tourists and homeless people also seemed to be drawn to this location. I couldn't figure it out at first, but then I realized why. For tourists, they wanted to get a Starbucks in their hot little mitts before they hit the streets of Manhattan. For the homeless, it was much simpler. It had a public bathroom.

I sipped and continued to watch the two girls as they prepared to leave. They chatted excitedly about their evening of shopping as they put their coats, gloves, and scarves on. Tourists, I thought. Far too happy to be New Yorkers, especially in the winter. Don't get me wrong. There is no doubt that New York City stands alone during the holiday season. The tree at Rockefeller Center, the windows at Macy's, Saint Patrick's

Cathedral, ice skating at Wollman Rink. Magical. Mid-February, not so magical. With twinkling lights gone and holiday music silenced, the city turns gray. Slush freezes and thaws and then freezes again, trapping within it bits and pieces of debris. The sidewalks are hastily scraped so that pedestrians can walk safely, everything pushed toward drainage grates. There, the filthy balls of ice will sit until it becomes warm enough for the lumps to melt, and that, my friend, is at least two months away. You can always tell who the native New Yorkers are, especially in February. They are the ones who are determined to grimace. At least until the spring thaw.

Finally, the girls stood up. They slung designer bags over their shoulders and walked for the exit. I swooped toward the table and didn't mind that it was dirty. The two girls had not disposed of their trash. But, I didn't care. I just wanted a place to sit. I plopped down and took a napkin from my pocket and wiped the table as best as I could. I pushed the trash to the edge of the table and placed my purse on the chair next to me. My plan was to save a seat for Gino. He was to meet me later that afternoon.

He had spent the day in Port Washington. If you don't know where that is, it is on Long Island. He was there for work and had left very early that morning to make the trip. And, what a trip it was. From our home on East 76th Street, Gino walked the three blocks to the 6 train subway stop on Lexington Avenue. From there, he traveled south to 51st Street. He then transferred to the E train, which took him to Penn Station. At Penn Station, he boarded the LIRR, a.k.a. Long Island Railroad, to make the rest of the journey to Port Washington. All told, his commute was just short of two hours. And, now, he was doing it again, in reverse.

When we spoke earlier that day, he asked if I would meet

him at Penn Station. There, we could have a coffee and then take the subway uptown together. It is so much nicer to ride the subway with someone rather than alone. Thus, my reason for being at Starbucks in Penn Station on a Tuesday afternoon in mid-February.

I settled back in my chair, content to sit, sip, and wait. I was at the very back of the restaurant and looked forward to people-watching until Gino arrived. His LIRR train was scheduled to get to Penn Station in about twenty minutes or so, but trains are often delayed, so it was hard to be sure.

I scanned the room. I first noticed her when she stepped into the restaurant. Tall, thin, twenty-ish. Clad in blue jeans and a thick red sweater, she walked toward the counter to place an order. As she studied the menu board, she took off her black stocking cap and put it in her backpack. Strands of her long hair stood up briefly. Static electricity.

She waited in line until it was her turn to order. She did and then moved to the other end of the counter to get her beverage. I lost her in the crowd and found myself looking at other people instead. But suddenly, she appeared again. She walked in my direction. I assumed she was going to the ladies' room, which was down a hallway just behind me. But, instead, she stopped at my table.

"Is that seat taken?" she pointed to the chair where I had placed my handbag. I really hate it when other people save seats for long periods of time, especially in such crowded places, so I removed my bag and indicated that she could sit down. She put her coffee cup down and reached to take her backpack off her shoulder. As she did, her cell phone rang. She hastily rummaged through her bag to answer her phone.

Before I write this next part, there is something you should know. I do not believe in eavesdropping. I don't think that it is ever appropriate to listen to someone else's private conversation. However, sometimes, it is unavoidable. Especially in this day and age. It is amazing to me what people talk about on their cell phones. Intimate details, private thoughts spoken aloud in very public places. It is as if they think that because they have plugged one of their ears with their pointer finger and pressed their cell phone firmly to the other ear, that no one can hear them. And, yet, quite the opposite is true, especially in a noisy environment. They speak even louder so that the person on the other end can hear, thereby providing those nearby with crystal-clear details of their conversation.

"Hello?" she said. After a brief pause, she continued. "Thank God you called back. I have so much to tell you." And so it started. After the first minute or so, I looked for another table to move to. No luck. I considered waiting outside the restaurant for Gino, but decided against it since I didn't know exactly how long he would be. Finally, I just resigned myself. I had no choice. I listened. For twenty minutes, I listened. As best as I could piece it together, here is her story.

She was at Starbucks because her train for Boston was delayed. At least an hour, she said to the person on the other end of the line. She couldn't wait to see this person, she said. Yes, it had been a long time and lots had happened. I assumed that she was talking to a high-school friend. By her comments, it seemed that she had not seen this friend since graduation, two years earlier. She had left Boston to come to New York to become an actress. And so her story poured out. Since she did most of the talking, I got a very accurate portrayal of her life.

After only a few months of living here, she knew that she wanted to go home. She didn't like the lifestyle; she didn't like her roommate. She took acting classes and went on auditions but felt very much out of place. The party scene was intense and she felt tremendous peer pressure to participate. After the first semester, she called her parents and asked to come home. They said it was normal to feel homesick and that she should stick it out. Besides, they had paid a tremendous amount of money for her education. None of it was refundable. So, she stayed.

To make herself feel a bit better, she partied just a little more. Not a lot, she said. Just enough to take the edge off and fit in with the crowd.

She continued her classes and went on auditions, but she just couldn't seem to book anything. Someone suggested that she needed a private acting coach, so she took a waitressing job to have the funds to hire a coach. After several months of coaching, she was still unable to get a job. She told her coach that she felt that acting wasn't really for her. Maybe the best thing to do was pack it in and go home. The coach said it took most actors several years to book their first big gig. That made sense, so she stayed on.

After her first year at school, she moved out of the dorms and in with a friend who had sublet an apartment. It was tiny and overrun with rats. The two had attached a bed sheet to the ceiling to create two separate sleeping areas. She barely got by. The money she made from waitressing covered only the rent and her coach. She was very unhappy. She told her roommate that she really just wanted to go home. But, the roommate said that she was responsible for half of the rent and, if she left, she would have to find someone to take over her part. She felt defeated by that notion, so she stayed.

Into her second year of school, she partied a bit more. But, it didn't really matter, anyway. Her grades had slipped and she still hadn't gotten any parts. Besides, her focus had shifted. She had met a guy. Several years older than her, he was the bartender where she waitressed. At first, she was very resistant to having sex with him, but eventually she gave in. She told him once that she really just wanted to go back to Boston. He said if she did, that it was over between them. So, once again, she stayed.

That's when she started to cry. Not wailing sobs, but crying, nonetheless. Until this point, I had avoided looking at her. I had positioned my chair so that I could continue to watch the people in the restaurant and not be forced into eye contact with her. For her part, she had kept her head mostly down. But now, I looked directly at her. Her long hair concealed most of her face, but I could still see tears as they streamed down her cheeks. Sensing that I was looking at her, it seemed that she realized for the first time how loud her voice had been. She glanced briefly at me and lowered her tone but continued her conversation. She said she just didn't know what to do. How could she possibly tell her parents, she asked. Yes, yes, she said. She was pretty sure she was....

She turned away abruptly. I wasn't able to hear anything else. She picked up her backpack and slung it over her shoulder and stood up. She looked around for a moment as if to get her bearings. Then, she put on her stocking cap and left. I watched her until she was swallowed up by the crowd. I pondered her final words. She was pretty sure she was.... what? I wondered. Pretty sure she was going to leave school whether her parents blessed her decision or not? Or, pretty sure she was pregnant? I would never know.

It was only a few more minutes before I spotted Gino. He had finally arrived. The restaurant was standing room only, so he just smiled broadly and waved. I waved back and motioned that I had saved a seat for him. He got in line to get his coffee and finally made his way over to the table. He sat down and told me about his day. Then, he asked me about mine. I told him about the girl and what I had overheard. And, how sad it made me. He looked at me and said nothing, just listened. And waited.

"I think it's time," I said. He nodded. He knew exactly what I was referring to and he agreed.

So there, amidst the tourists and homeless of New York City, in a Starbucks coffeehouse on the lower level of Penn Station, I resigned from QVC. In my mind, it was over. Better to step off into the abyss of the unknown than stay somewhere I knew I no longer belonged.

We sealed our decision with a coffee-flavored kiss, gathered our belongings, and made our way to the E train. As we walked, I realized that the stocking-cap girl was already leaving my mind. But before she evaporated completely, I silently prayed that, before it was too late, she would give herself permission to leave. Permission to be. Permission to find her own happiness.

I finally had.

Big Life Lesson Number Ten: When it comes to 'moving on', the only permission you really need is God's.

CONCLUSION

So, there they are. My big life lessons. Not exactly earth shattering, but mine, nonetheless.

If you take nothing else from this little text, I hope it is this: I hope this book will prompt you to sit down and write your own life lessons. I hope it will encourage you to think of the people and places and events in your life and how God has worked in each. I hope you will realize that both joyful and shameful occurrences can provide valuable lessons.

And if, by chance, you don't have any life lessons yet, don't panic. Remember, you don't have to be a minister, a missionary, or an expert to learn from God. You only have to listen. So, just listen. Because, He is still out there. He still loves you. And, He is still speaking.

Revelation 3:20: ...if any man hear my voice, and open the door, I will come in to him...

ACKNOWLEGMENTS

Thank you to Big Mike for allowing me to mention his film. Please visit www.IronCityBlues.com for more information.

LaVergne, TN USA
20 March 2011
220845LV00002B/190/P